AN
ACTOR'S
LIFE
FOR
ME?

AN ACTOR'S LIFE FOR ME?

ZOE CUNNINGHAM

HOW TO GET STARTED IN ACTING

URBANE
Publications

urbanepublications.com

First published in Great Britain in 2017
by Urbane Publications Ltd
Suite 3, Brown Europe House, 33/34 Gleaming Wood Drive,
Chatham, Kent ME5 8RZ
Copyright © Zoe Cunningham, 2017

A CIP catalogue record for this book is available
from the British Library.

ISBN 978-1-911129-72-1
MOBI 978-1-911129-74-5
EPUB 978-1-911129-73-8

Design and Typeset by Michelle Morgan

Cover by Julie Martin

Printed and bound by CPI Group (UK) Ltd, Croydon, CR0 4YY

urbanepublications.com

To Peta and Jeremy who nurtured me when I was only a sapling; to Marianna who made me a film star; and to my husband Sean who believed in me enough for two of us.

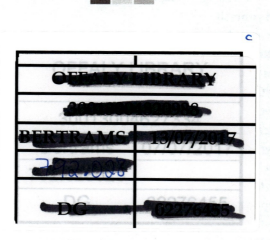

CONTENTS

AN ACTOR'S LIFE FOR ME

INTRODUCTION

Acting is a hard path to take. The life of an actor is a difficult one. It is filled with heartbreak, despair, joy and hope. It is easy to become consumed by the despair and the heartbreak until you break through that and bask in the joy. The whole process of becoming an actor is an intense version of living, with extreme emotions tumbling one after another. This is one of the reasons that people who start down the path rarely lose it from their hearts. When you are acting you are really alive.

Like many young people, I was dissuaded from acting as a child, and firmly instructed in what is required to be successful in the real world. Unlike some I did not have enough belief in acting to defy my parents and do it anyway. This is not a regret. I am very grateful to my parents for this sound grounding, which has made me self-sufficient in my life. Coming to acting later in life means that I can approach it as a good in itself, rather than a means of defining myself as a person, or of earning a living. Creativity thrives when it is free and struggles when it is limited by expectations. Having to earn a living from your creativity can often kill it outright.

I have now been acting for two years. It is still hard, and I face many challenges and self-doubts. But no point on the acting journey is as hard as the absolute start of it. We live today in an impatient society, where we want everything immediately. We have lost the patience to build things slowly over time, and we have replaced it with instant dopamine hits from online news feeds. The skill of acting does not respond well to this "must have it now" approach. Opinions vary (and you will hear some opposing ones in the interviews I have included in the book) on how much of acting is nature rather than nurture, but it is hard to not start the journey by questioning whether you even ought to attempt it. Further it's hard to find the answer to be "yes" when you compare your nascent acting ability to the very visible actors with tens of years of experience.

There is a popular career choosing model that you should find the intersection of "what you are good at", "what you love" and "what is useful for other people". This pre-supposes that you will already be good at the thing you are destined to do. Having gone through my acting journey I see no reason to assume that should be the case. When I started acting I was not good at it. I was terrible. I was terrible in the same way that a child learning to walk, or talk, or do anything, is terrible. I was wooden, because I was terrified by the whole exposure in front of people. I was inflexible, because I had little experience of different approaches. I was lucky that some people saw some "talent" in me. Many did not.

I don't think I would have been able to sustain the effort needed for two years had I not found a deep connection to acting through a book that I read almost by accident (The Artist's Way by Julia Cameron). The belief that I could do it keep me going through the constant rejections and abysmal performances. It kept me going when I cried at failed auditions and at the apparent demise of a project that I was pinning all my hopes on. Looking back, I realise how easy it would have been to stop at those points, declare that I had no talent and to quit. It is only because I didn't quit that I am still here two years later. It's only because I didn't give up that I have found the feeling that maybe I could be good at this after all.

I have spent two years learning how to learn to be an actor. Before I started I had no idea that it was possible to learn in this way, and to have fantastic experiences with other film and theatre makers who were also on a journey to learn more about their own respective crafts. There are things that I have done in these two years that I did not, in my heart of hearts, believe I could achieve: producing and acting in a short film, getting cast in an independent feature film, getting an agent, having an audition for a TV show... the list is extensive.

I still have a long way to go. That is one of the challenges of acting. The road is hard, and it is also long. But I've learnt that it can be walked, simply by continually putting one foot in front of another, no matter how much despair you feel. I've learnt that it's worth walking, even if you don't get to the end.

These two beliefs are my cornerstones of how to become an actor.

1. Anyone can become an actor, just by starting and keeping going.
2. Acting is worthwhile even if you don't earn a living from it.

In this book, I share my approach to learning how to act. I hope that it can be useful for you as you learn to act. I hope you find the courage to start small and count the many small wins you will encounter. I hope you find the strength to keep going. And I hope you find it to be as fulfilling, rewarding and fun as I have.

Zoe Cunningham

A NON-ACTOR'S LIFE

Like many people, some who are now professional actors and many who are not, I was part of several acting groups when I was younger. In fact I did a lot of things, like lots of children – life saving swimming, gymnastics, violin lessons, ballet. Apart from an initial desire to be a ballerina (I somehow imbibed the idea that this was the ideal of all womanhood) the childhood activity that really resonated with me was acting. I loved it.

Like many childhood loves, I loved acting but I wasn't sure that acting loved me back. I wanted to be a part of it with all my heart, but I always felt somehow out of place. I was painfully shy and I felt that that meant that maybe acting wasn't for me. But I loved it so much that I persisted.

I think that it was as the shy quiet girl desperately trying to fit in that I picked up a lot of misconceptions about acting that remained with me until relatively recently. I felt that being good at acting was linked with popularity and being loud and having people look at you all the time (not just when you were on stage). I might also have stretched to saying that acting was about learning lines but

I knew deep down it was more than that. It was some ineffable quality that some people had and some people didn't. I was very clear on that. Some small spark of hope persisted and I bumbled along through several groups and very minor parts in many plays, but I was never trying to improve my skills and get better, only hoping that I would wake up one day and discover that, yes, it was me! I had been one of these special people all along! and now I knew it was true because I'd been given the lead and everyone loved me and I was amazing.

Needless to say, that wasn't what happened. I persisted in tentatively auditioning for things throughout my school years and the roles that I did get didn't make me feel that I was destined for acting. In the fifth form I was cast in Midsummer's Night's Dream (hooray), but as a fairy (one line – "And me."). Worse, I was cast alongside three first years as a humorously large fairy. I can still feel the pain of that to this day. In the sixth form I was cast in a small but perfectly formed role in the school production of Nicholas Nickleby, only to have the director realise in our first rehearsal that my part had been cut not only from that scene but from the entire play.

I did have a lovely role as Addaperle, The Good Witch of the North, in the Wiz, where my nerves about acting were calmed by the fact I was mostly singing rather than speaking and also by the fact that I was carried offstage by my friend Polly's hot boyfriend (I was especially delighted when Polly told me to "Watch it!" and that I'd "Better not try anything!"). The director was my best friend Debbie, so I suspect at least a certain amount of nepotism in the selection. Even though I felt I did a good job, landing the role didn't give me that sense of recognition by the universe that I craved.

My parents were very clear in their views of acting as a career. Namely that it wasn't one. I was told in no uncertain terms that it was not possible to earn money as an actor, and that I should focus on doing well at school and going on to university. Of course, I now realise that my parents were absolutely 100% correct, and I think they missed a trick. I think that more and more the world is won by people who focus on more than one thing, who don't let themselves be put into a single box and stay there.

My mother was also worried about the heartache involved in being an actor. The constant trying and failing, of feeling like you're not good enough. Now that I'm giving it a go I've found that she was 100% right on that too. But I've learnt a different attitude and that it's how you get through the heartache that's important, not how you avoid it. Would 17-year-old me have been able to cope? We'll never know. (But my guess is no.)

Like many of Britain's greatest actors and comedians – Emma Thompson, Steven Fry, Sue Perkins & Mel Giedroyc, Simon Munnery and most of Monty Python – I was lucky enough to attend Cambridge University. What an opportunity! Unlike all of the above however, I did no creative pursuits, met none of the other amazing actors/directors/creatives of the future and totally wasted my time there. I didn't apply to the illustrious Footlights, indeed I was only dimly aware that it existed.

Instead I spent three years solidly engaged in drinking, partying, armchair philsophising and playing board games. Not only did I not put a lot of effort into my mathematics degree, but I didn't do much else productive either. I've since met people who wrote books or worked on plays in their time at uni. I even met one guy who managed to shoot his first feature film while he was studying at Oxford. Why wasn't I doing that??

I've met people with two types of regret about their time in education. Firstly, there are those who regret not studying harder when they had the chance. I do have some slight sympathy for that position now. I've come to realise that if you're going to spend a large amount of time on something, you may as well put your heart and soul into it and get what you can from it instead of engaging half-heartedly and wishing you were somewhere else. But on the flip side, I've also met a lot of people who regret *having worked too hard* when they were at university. "If only I'd known then how little what grade I got would matter when I got into the real world, I might have lived a little rather than constantly studying."

If I'm honest I feel I totally got the amount of work right. Doing the minimum was a good call. But I really, really regret not spending my time on something more engaging. I was 20 years old with masses of free time. How much more fun could I have had shooting even a terrible short or putting on an amateur play?

Scraping through my degree did get me my first "proper job". I'd mucked about a bit coding on a ZX Spectrum (remember? the one with the rubber keys?) when I was a child and so when I was contacted by a software development agency, I thought that might be a reasonable job to pursue. I went for an interview, discovered that the software industry was laid back and straightforward (win!) and took the job almost without thinking about it. Writing software wasn't my big dream for my life, but like almost everyone else in the world I needed a job.

The first six years in my software job were very typical of so many people in the working world. I dragged myself out of bed to go to work. I tried to get the things done that I had to before someone noticed, while exerting as little effort as possible. I learned how many cigarette breaks it was possible to take in one day without looking like you're taking the piss. Outside of work I had parties, and went drinking and thought that was what life was about.

I had vague ideas that I would like to be promoted. I wrote this in my appraisal every year, and didn't take any further actions towards that goal. I had the same dreams that we all have from time to time, that if only I could give up work and party full time, life would be amazing.

In the middle of this, the universe gave me a sign. I read an interview with Catherine Zeta-Jones in a women's magazine. It said that Zeta-Jones had suffered from terrible shyness as a child, but had worked hard to get over it so that she could pursue her love of acting. That caught my attention. I had been shy as a child, and I had reacted the only way I thought was possible, by feeling sad about it and giving up on what I wanted to do. I could see that Catherine-Zeta Jones' response was much, much smarter than mine.

I ignored this sign from the universe. I was 23 years old. I can remember that because I remember thinking "Ha! It's OK for Catherine Zeta-Jones, who realised this when she was a child. I'm 23 years old so now I'm far too old to do anything about it." Starting out as an actor aged 35, I find it terribly amusing (and heartbreakingly sad) to think back on that reaction.

Instead I carried on with my job in software. I was starting to feel that it wasn't working out for me, as I was passed over for promotion time and time again for my more hardworking colleagues. I could feel that something was wrong, but I didn't know what it was. I just knew that I had to do something different before life slipped away from me.

My husband then got a really great job offer. He worked for an Australian company and had helped them to set up the UK operations. They were keen to fly him out to Australia for an eighteen-month secondment so that they could share knowledge between Australia and the UK. My husband wasn't sure whether he should accept this offer. I was jumping up and down for him to take it. This was the change I was looking for in my life! Anything could happen in Australia.

While I was convincing my husband that he should take the job, I also spent some time thinking what I would do. We lived in Willesden Green at the time, with a large antipodean population working in the local bars. That was it! I could move to Australia and be a Brit (Pom, in Australian terminology) working in the bars of Sydney.

As I was working up to telling my employers that I had to quit, I had another idea. The world of software development is modern and employee-friendly. The reason that I feared speaking with my employers is that I felt it would make them sad if I left. But now we have the internet, maybe I could do some programming remotely?

I planned my "pitch". I explained how I didn't want to have to leave the company, but that my husband had this amazing offer in Australia. I tentatively suggested that maybe I could carry on working for the company, but just remotely. My boss asked for some time to consider my request. When he got back to me he explained their thinking as follows. "We have a slight preference for you to be in the office in the UK, but it's only a slight one." I was free to go.

I had been sure that my life would change if I started a new venture or changed career. I was pleased to have a job to take with me to Australia, but I didn't expect it to change my life dramatically in the way it might have if I had been forced to start again. But life can have a funny way of giving you what you need. In the end I learnt far more by staying with the same job in different circumstances. The things that I learnt while working remotely were the start of a change in the direction of my life.

While I was in Australia, I had a big lesson in "self-efficacy" (I learnt the word later!). Let me explain a bit about my working pattern before I went to Australia. You first need to know that software development is quite hard and consists mostly of finding that what you have done doesn't work in some mysterious way. You are constantly trying to find and diagnose problems that you weren't expecting.

This diagram sums it up!

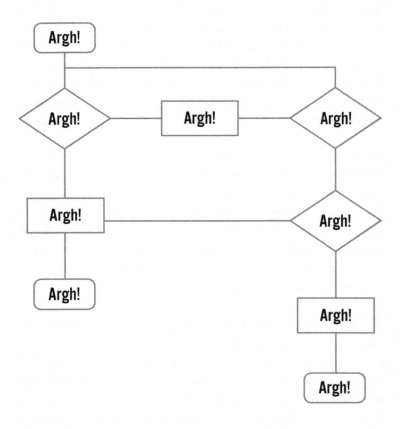

The company where I learnt how to code was very good at training us in efficiency. It is no good to be spending several days struggling with something if someone can give you the answer in 5 minutes. I picked up this tip really quickly and applied it well. Too well, it turned out. I had developed a pattern whereby when I hit an issue I would stare blankly at my screen for the requisite amount of time until I felt I had "tried long enough to solve it", then ask my friend Matthew what the answer was. Using this approach I was a reasonably successful programmer.

When I went to Australia, everything changed. Well, one thing in particular changed. Whenever I hit a problem, Matthew was asleep. The first day, I opened up my computer, started coding a web component and bam, 10am, problem. I did the first thing I always did when I hit a problem, I made a cup of tea. Then I stared blankly at the screen for a bit. Then I realised that I couldn't call Matthew to solve the problem. I stared at the screen a bit more. When my brain realised that it had to solve the problem itself it stared a little less blankly. It started to engage with the problem. And sure enough three hours later, it had solved it. A little disappointing compared to the five minutes that Matthew would have taken but very exciting and illuminating to realise that it had been done 100% by me.

This simple act of solving my own problem gave me a big realisation. I had been telling myself that I couldn't solve these problems. I had believed that there was something special or different about how Matthew's brain worked which was why I couldn't do it. In Australia, I realised that I just hadn't been trying. As I worked through more and more things on my own, I got quicker. (Not as quick as Matthew, but significantly quicker than I had been.) I learnt that I had more control over my environment than I had previously thought. I started to believe in my own self-efficacy.

It turns out whether you think you will eventually succeed when you do something makes a big difference to whether you decide to start it, and whether you stick with it when the going gets tough. (The going always gets tough at some point.) So although this learning had nothing to do with the field of acting, without it I don't think I would be here, still trying to become an actor after two years. I would have dropped out after the first painful audition, or I would have gradually "forgotten" to do it or I would have let myself off the hook completely by "realising that I don't have any talent". What I realised in Australia is that you have to try.

When I came back to the UK I found a very simple application for this learning. When I give talks at events on my career I feel embarrassed explaining the "new belief" that I tried out that made all the difference to how successful I was at my job. It's something that many people have absolutely no problem applying, but which for some reason took me six years to discover. I came back to London and I decided that I would try "being good at my job" i.e. trying hard and seeing where I got to. This had never occurred to me before.

Seeing the change that this made to how successful I was in my job has caused me to re-evaluate what the most important criteria are for success in the world. I believed in talent and aptitude, but now I think that attitude and beliefs are much more important. With my new way of working, I went from writing the same goal in my appraisal every year that I didn't hit, to setting and hitting successively higher goals every single year. Everything suddenly seemed easy.

After a few years of this I felt so confident that I sat down and worked out my own career plan. What if I set my sights even higher? What if I set a goal that would run over years rather than months? I sat down one Saturday morning in 2010 and worked out a plan. In 2012 (sooner even than I had hoped) I was appointed as the first Managing Director of my company. Yay! I didn't know it then, but these were building blocks one and two for starting to learn to be an actor. One: I now had a well-paid and flexible job. Two: I had learned how to sustain long term effort to achieve bigger goals.

In 2009, a big change happened in the world of television. Carol Vorderman parted ways with Countdown. This may have gone unnoticed by all but stalwart Countdown fans, but for me it suddenly seemed like a great opportunity. I had a mathematics degree and wanted to be on the telly. I could be the next Countdown numbers lady! Channel 4 issued a notice to say that they were accepting open applications from across the country. The winner would get a full-time job and a salary of £100,000!

I sent straight off for the application form and worked hard on putting my answers together. I'd already managed to get interviewed on my friend's TV show The World Series of Backgammon, so I asked for the clips of my interview and sent it off with my application as a proto-showreel. I was really excited about the application. I wondered what the audition process would be like. I envisioned some kind of fake Countdown set where I would pretend to be Carol and get videoed answering numbers questions.

I felt that I had quite a good chance with my application. I had a mathematics degree and I had TV experience! I sent off my form and waited to hear back. And waited. And waited. It was an application procedure that I now know well, but had not encountered at that time. You know the one where if you don't hear back you didn't get it. I kept waiting hopefully. Then I worried that maybe my email didn't get through. I drafted a chasing email.

Then I thought better of it and didn't send it. What if they were just about to reply to me and my email put them off?

I can't remember if I was still waiting by the time that they announced that Rachel Riley had got the job, but I remained disappointed that I hadn't even got an audition. They hadn't seen what I could do! I went through the (at the time new, but now so familiar!) post-mortem process of wondering what I did wrong. Were my three words to describe myself just not the right ones? I did say "fun" didn't I? Maybe at 29 I was considered too old? (The fact that Riley was fresh out of university confirmed this theory to me!) A friend suggested that I was physically too similar to Carol Vorderman and that they would be looking to cast someone with a completely different look.

Whatever the reason, that was it, I was not to start a glittering career as a TV presenter. I moped a little bit (just a little bit) and complained to my husband. My husband's response astounded me. "You don't need them! You can make your own Countdown!" What?! How? I didn't know any TV people or how to get a show onto a major TV channel. I didn't have a format or any idea about what I was doing. It was a great supportive suggestion from my husband but I had no idea where to start with it. Then he gave me a slightly modified one that I could work with. "Well we know Andy who makes World Series of Backgammon, maybe you can do some presenting for him?"

Encouraged by my husband, who needed to explain precisely each step to me in order for me to know what to do, I made a grainy test video of me interviewing a few backgammon players at a local event. The sound was horrible and it looked pretty scrappy but I sent it off anyway. And imagine my joy – I got a positive response! Perhaps not exactly the response I was looking for – "Zoe I think you are destined to be a star and I would be honoured to have you on my show" – instead Andy told me kindly that he was looking for someone to help with administration at the event, and if I'd be happy to take a job helping behind the organiser's desk, I could have time off to have a go at presenting when it was convenient for the organisation.

Not having any experience in this area, and somewhat launching myself in, I was rather astounded to discover that being a presenter was an awesome job and that I would love to do more of it. After watching back the World Series of Backgammon videos several (a-hem) times, I immediately started looking for ways to apply to be a presenter for other organisations and get more experience. This was my first experience with an "in demand" creative role. I was used to working in software development where the number of jobs outstrips the number of people available to do them. In technology people are desperate to hire you if you are trained, and very often they will take you even if you aren't, and they themselves will pay to train you. This was how I became a software developer to start with.

So I was struck by the stark contrast in presenting. I was an inexperienced and "OK" presenter and yet even getting unpaid work experience seemed to be close to impossible. I applied for an unpaid student TV project and lost the gig to a dance teacher who thought presenting might be fun.

While I failed to get any non-backgammon jobs, "working" in the backgammon world was going really well. Having made some contacts with camera people through the World Series of Backgammon, my husband and I started make our own online backgammon shows to cover backgammon events in the UK and Europe. One of my favourite jokes is that I am the top European backgammon presenter. (In case my joke isn't clear, I'm only top because there aren't any others!)

One thing I did discover while trying hard to break into the mainstream was that there are lots and lots of extremely kind people in this industry who are happy to help you out. I had many meetings with executives at production companies and employees of the BBC who constantly gave me the same message – get an expertise and create content around that.

I was a bit confused by this advice to start with as it was exactly what I was doing with my backgammon expertise. The challenge was that backgammon was not mainstream enough – how many backgammon shows do you see on TV? When I thought around the subject a bit I realised that I had another expertise that I had been missing all along. Technology.

Starting to rebrand myself as a technology expert and chasing down every contact I could make at the BBC led to my favourite presenting credit – I did an interview with the amazing tech charity Tiger Nation for technology show BBC Click on the BBC Worldwide radio channel. I was a presenter on the BBC!

Writing this summary looking backwards sounds really simple and straightforward. I feel I must point out that this progress took me about five years from when I did my first presenting for the World Series of Backgammon. And one BBC credit is not enough to suddenly launch you into the mainstream. As I pursued presenting I was finding that although I loved some aspects of it, I was constantly building up a "to do" list of things that I didn't really want to do, but I felt would be good for getting ahead: blogging, research, cold calling and many more. I had had lots of great opportunities, but it hadn't really turned into everything I was hoping for.

This is where I was at in March 2014. I'd had a great year in 2013. Through the random chances that come up in life I'd started the year being placed second on a BBC show called Britain's Brightest, and ended the year by going to China on a trade mission with the Prime Minister. So I'd started 2014 feeling that 2013 couldn't be topped and what was I doing with my life anyway?

It turns out that what I had been doing was perfectly preparing to be an actor. It might not look like it at first glance but the universe had helped me to create several key building blocks that are now essential for me to be able to pursue acting.

Flexible job. I hadn't been working in an acting or performance related job. But I had built myself up a role in a well-paid field that supports flexible working. Many actors are forced to take corporate or commercial jobs just to pay the bills, when being a commercial actor wasn't their aim when they started out. Or they have to take low-paid and insecure roles such as waiting tables. My job in a completely unrelated field is still a big asset to me.

Camera experience. Presenting isn't acting (I once had this argument with a casting director in one of my first auditions, who said that presenting was quite similar in some ways and I argued against it – while suddenly realising that this wasn't one of my smartest moves!!!) but having extensive experience in front of a camera has definitely come in handy.

Doing it yourself. It is possible that in the golden era of the 1950s you could build a career as an actor and always be working in other people's productions. Even if it was true then, it is definitely no longer true now. Being able to be the instigator and make things happen is absolutely critical if you want to act.

Perseverance. Trying to make my way in presenting was just as tough as it is now as an actor. In many ways it was even more tough, as in my heart of hearts I wasn't sure it was what I wanted to do. This, plus building up my career in my day job taught me how all worthwhile things are built up over time, not just "found" overnight.

Life experience. At the most basic level, acting is about portraying life. Every extra year you live, you build up life experience. Every new thing you do expands your repertoire of what you can portray. Never underestimate this!

I've read in many books that we all follow an individual path. It took me a while to understand what was meant by this. My model of the world, derived from my experience in our academic system, is that there is a "proper way" to do things and a set way to get to a certain end. It turns out that life is not like that at all. There are many ways to skin a cat (or indeed do something more pleasant). This is even more true with acting, a skill where there are almost as many different theories of practice as there are practitioners and where even those who are at the top in the profession can't concisely explain exactly what it is that they do.

If you have a desire to act, that is a message from the universe. And if the universe is telling you to do something, it will have been helping you out with circumstances and coincidences to enable you to achieve that end. I didn't always think like this, but then again, I wasn't always an actor.

Interview – Sarah Campbell

Sarah Campbell is an accomplished solicitor, a director and an actor. She's managed to build a "normal" career alongside directing and acting in plays around the world.

"I always wanted to be an actor. Sort of always. It was the only thing that ever made sense to me. Still is. I didn't really think about it though – I went to a very academic school, and was pushed around. They did speaking rather than acting. I left in the sixth form and went to another school where I did theatre studies A-level and joined the theatre club. I also joined the Belgrade Youth Theatre in Coventry.

Over the years I've done bits of training, at the Actors Centre on weekends. It's difficult to get an agent unless you go through drama school and agents come to see you. I tried to get an agent and went to drama school auditions, but they wanted different things from what I could offer. I still acted, for example I toured Shakespeare round Europe. Then I stopped for 15 years when I had children. I was pouring all my creativity into my children so it was difficult to do any theatre.

Then one day when my children were mid-teens, I just went off for an audition. I thought 'How have I not had this in my life for all those years?' When I went for this audition, I had to walk across the stage. They were building the set and I had to pick my way over everything in my heels. On the way back I suddenly realised that I was on a stage, looking out across the auditorium. And it was like I'd forgotten who I was for 15 years – like a vampire that had forgotten I was a vampire and then tasted blood.

It makes sense of everything when I'm in a play, but it doesn't pay anything. You can still act of course. I work with many semi-professional companies. You have a day job and rehearse in the evenings. The plays are done as profit-share – I've actually made money from plays. There is a whole other strata. If you want to do it, you can do it. Get some people together, make a play and hit the festivals. You can make a little bit or lose a little bit of money.

I've also worked with amateur groups, which is very interesting. There is lots more of a mix in London – elsewhere in the country you just have amateur groups. They are amazing; they have little theatres where they make a profit putting on 5-6 plays/year. But their comfort zone isn't very deep, so they very often get to a place where they wouldn't go any further. It's much more exciting to work with people who want to learn and who want to push themselves."

THE ARTIST'S WAY

I started 2014 on a low. I had had an amazing 2013, but both of my favourite experiences – coming second in Britain's Brightest and going to China with the Prime Minister – came about by chance. I didn't have a formula for how to replicate them. I had no idea how I could set myself exciting goals for 2014 that I could actually make happen.

I had plenty of angles still to pursue for presenting. In fact I had a big long "to do" list of ideas that could be helpful for my presenting career. I could write and present a science podcast, or a technology podcast or an "interesting things about the world" podcast. I had the contact details of many people who I suspected were not at all interested in working with me for me to email and introduce myself to. I had blog articles to write to "get my name out there". I had a million and one things to do, but I didn't want to do any of them.

In March I went on holiday to Morocco with my husband. As was now my style, I took my to do list away with me, so that I could get some things done in all this free time. My body thought differently. I came down with a bug and was sick for two days. I didn't even

look at my to do list. I finished the novel that I was reading and looked around for another book on my Kindle app.

A friend who had just started writing her first novel had recommended a book called The Artist's Way to me. In fact, I'm not sure she really recommended it at all – she just said in a short email "Reading the Artist's Way and it's great." I had taken this as a recommendation and, not knowing at all what the book was about, had bought a Kindle copy to read later.

As I flicked through my unread books, lying on an ottoman with a blanket over me, The Artist's Way caught my eye. A book for unblocking creative people. Pah! I wasn't creative. I was a science and technology person. For some reason I decided to read it anyway. This was the book that changed the direction of my life.

Julia Cameron, the author of The Artist's Way, was a journalist and screenwriter when she wrote The Artist's Way in 1992. In the 70s she was married to Martin Scorsese, and hung around with Steven Spielberg. One of the things that I like about the book is that you don't find out about her Hollywood friends until right at the end – she's just another person like you all the way through the book.

The Artist's Way contains a twelve-week course based on classes that Cameron taught in California. Each week there are some essays to read about different aspects of creativity and some exercises to do. Some of the exercises are clearly of an unblocking nature, for example "Draw five pictures of other careers that you might have had." Some are less obvious but I think they do unblock you in a subtle way. My favourite example is one that made my husband laugh out loud at me – "Collect five pretty stones this week."

AN ACTOR'S LIFE FOR ME

I loved having little tasks to do each week. It felt really positive and each one was something that I could happily do. Through following The Artist's Way I rediscovered drawing, baking and craft. I found myself doing and enjoying the things that I had loved as a child and yet stopped pursuing as an adult because "there's never enough time".

There are two fundamental exercises from The Artist's Way that you continue with even after you finish the book. The first is called Morning Pages. The Morning Pages are three written pages of longhand that you do every day. I find the rules for the Morning Pages very interesting. You are allowed to write anything you like. You can write "I don't know what to write." over and over again until you have filled three pages. The only rule is that you have to do three pages every day. I have written Morning Pages every single day (with one exception, when I was on holiday and spent most of the day asleep and forgot) since I started the Artist's Way in March 2014.

The Morning Pages are really just an example of journaling, which is very popular with positive psychology help books at the moment. I think there are two main benefits. One is learning how to get past your inner critic and just get stuff out and on to the page. The other is to have a place where you can pour out all the crap that you feel about the world, and about other people, without having it exposed to any scrutiny. (You are not allowed to ever show your Morning Pages to another person.)

Julia Cameron warns in her book that the second exercise is much harder than the Morning Pages. This exercise is called an Artist Date, and you must do one once every week for two hours. Unlike my strict adherence to the Morning Page, I have not done an Artist Date every week since starting The Artist's Way. I think I have done more than 50%, but even looking at my recent record, having just been very busy with a play, I did my first Artist Date this week having not done one for three weeks or so.

The Artist Date seems like it should be really easy. Again there are only a few constraints. You simply need to set aside two hours every week in order to do something fun. This should not be something that you are doing to advance your career (so if you are an actor, going to an acting class would not count, but attending a pottery workshop would) and you must do it on your own. The idea is that it is a date between you and your "inner artist".

I find that the fact that we all find the Artist Date difficult to be an interesting commentary on modern life. We are all so busy with jobs, and looking after families, and pursuing other goals that we cannot find two hours each week to spend on ourselves.

Julia Cameron insists that although it is hard to fit in, the Artist's Date is the most important exercise in the Artist's Way. She likens our creative resources to a fish pond. When we are writing, or drawing or otherwise creating, we are fishing from our fish pond. Cameron suggests that by engaging in a playful Artist's Date you are "restocking the fish pond". If you simply work and work and work you will run out of fish.

I can see that an Artist Date is useful for all kinds of reasons. It helps us to stop taking ourselves so seriously. It helps us to have some fun and engage our subconscious in our lives without yelling at it to perform. (There is a lovely quote from another creative coaching lady, Elizabeth Gilbert, best-selling author of Eat Pray Love. In her book Big Magic, she says "To yell at your creativity, saying 'You must earn money for me!' is sort of like yelling at a cat; it has no idea what you're talking about, and all you're doing is scaring it away, because you're making really loud noises and your face looks weird when you do that.") Utilising play and making sure you have fun with your life is definitely an important trait if you want to pursue a creative career. It's one that I'm still working on!

If you are considering reading the Artist's Way, there is one facet of the book that I feel I must warn you about. Cameron's whole explanation of our creativity and our duty to share our creative talents rests firmly on her deep religious conviction. She starts the book by saying that you just need to be open minded and that you can substitute whatever words you like for God. You can call Him "the great creator" or "the universe". I had just got my head around this when – bam! – exercise 1 "Recite the following prayer…"

As I continued through the book I became quite comfortable with this aspect of Cameron's belief. I now realise that a lot of the concepts that she is trying to convey – faith, hope and keeping going against the odds – are quite hard to explain against a purely rational backdrop. If you want to have the strength to keep going with acting when the times are tough, belief that a higher power has ordained this as the path for you to follow can be very reassuring. YMMV.

I faithfully followed the exercises laid out for me each week and eagerly read Cameron's descriptions of the creative process. I recognised so many in my own life: the Creative U-turn, where you start to find success and immediately retreat; the lack of satisfaction that you find in success if it wasn't what your heart wanted to achieve; and the delicacy of our new creative ideas if they are not immediately given nourishment and support (rather than criticism and attack).

I was enjoying the Artist's Way but I didn't know where I was headed. Then I had a very strong emotional reaction that I now see was the start of my unblocking. I went to the cinema to watch that 2014 filmic classic – The Lego Movie. As I was watching the trailers (I believe it was a trailer for Spiderman), I suddenly felt tears come to my eyes with an immense longing to be in films. It was an extremely unusual experience and I noted it down and carried on with my life.

It all made sense after I completed the exercise in week 8. In week 8 I was asked to write down what I would like to be doing in an ideal world. The exercise was to write down in as much detail as possible, what an ideal day in my ideal life would look like. Up until this point I had only vague ideas about what I wanted to do. I might have said that I would like to give up work, or become a TV presenter but they were only vague ideas rather than something specific.

It was at this point that I realised that the Artist's Way had really worked for me. It had unblocked me. Because as I was asked this question, I realised that I had an extremely detailed and specific answer. I wanted to be a film actor, and to live somewhere warm with great views with my husband. It was suddenly really easy to do and I knew it was what I really wanted. If I had been asked to answer this question before I read the book I would have floundered. I probably would have been able to put together an answer, but it would not have been convincing.

Looking back it seems crazy to me that I had no idea prior to this that I should be looking into acting. My third "sign from the universe that I ignored" had been a small part in a Michael Winterbottom film (The Look of Love, starring Steve Coogan and Anna Friel). A journalist had dropped out of the film the day before and I got a call from a friend (because his friend was a runner on the film) saying "Zoe, you're a journalist, aren't you?". Michael Winterbottom likes to cast the incidental roles with people who really work in those professions, rather than actors, and my TV presenting was sufficient to qualify me to play a newspaper reporter. I loved being on the film and I would have given anything to be a "proper actor" like Anna Friel, but I hadn't seen it as something I could pursue. Acting was for other people. Well, no longer!

The next exercise in the Artist's Way was to find some small steps that I could pursue, while not giving up my day job or turning my life upside down, in order to get me started on this path. Julia Cameron had spent a lot of time talking about how you didn't need to throw everything you had already away in order to embark on a creative career and how having a day job is a valuable asset. That made finding a next step really easy for me. I needed to look for classes and performing groups that I could fit around my day job.

Did I mention that one of Julia Cameron's big ideas is that when you are supposed to be doing something, the universe will help you out? As I was thinking of where to go for classes, I remembered that a year or two before my colleague and friend Szilvia Lukacs had been taking acing classes at City Lit University and she had recommended that I do them too. (Another message from the universe that I ignored at the time!) I got straight back in touch with her and found out how to book. I booked in a class for July and another one for August.

I was keen that as well as learning I also start performing. I reasoned that a good step would be to join an amateur dramatics company. A quick Google showed me that there were hundreds of companies in London. I picked the ten or so closest to me and joined their mailing lists.

Something that I picked up from my software job is that training is not the same thing as doing the job. Everyone I work with has spent three years at university training but now has to relearn everything in a work environment. As I embarked on acting, I was keen to carry that knowledge over. As I've worked through many different classes with many different organisations (RADA have some great classes for "over 24s". I enjoy being classified as an "over 24".) I've met people who have become quite trapped in taking classes. They never quite manage to make the leap over into becoming a performer rather than a dabbler.

If, like me, you're keen to get performing, classes where there is a performance as part of the class can be a fantastic way to get started. One of the initial two classes that I booked at City Lit was called "From the page to the stage" and involved four half day classes followed by a rehearsed reading of a play.

The Actor's Centre does a fabulous course called "Script to screen" where you train in screen acting for a few days and then act in a short film over the remaining days of the course. A great way to get showreel footage, your first short film credit and some training and experience! The film that I made as part of this course still forms the bulk of my showreel and shored up my early IMDB (Internet Movie Database) profile. We had a great director, Nicholas Cohen, and I'm still in touch with him and we have worked together on subsequent projects. (You can read the interview with Nick later in the book.)

Another great "train and act" course that I did was Colin Watkeys' Solo Theatre course. Acting in a one-person show is a great way to get experience and it's very accessible. Colin Watkeys is the master of this artform. He is always keen to explain that it is a form of theatre (hence the title "Solo Theatre") rather than an alternative to it. On Colin's course I learnt not only about performance but also about creating my own work and being prepared to perform it.

Whatever classes you decide you'd like to try, it's really important that you know what you want to get from them. We all grew up in a school system that operated like an escalator. You learn in one year, then you automatically proceed to the next level until you pop off the top and onto the job escalator. As I'm sure you have discovered through your life path, real life just doesn't work like that. If you're going to invest your time in learning how to act, as well as using all your energy earning a living doing something else, it's worth taking responsibility for what you want to learn and directing your training towards where you want to go.

I'm still taking classes, but I now take fewer general classes and more specialised courses. I've just started taking improvisation classes with Monkey Toast. They're not a school for training actors, but they are the experts in improvisation, which is an area that I'd like to improve in. Another class that I'd love to do when I find one that fits with my schedule is a class around movement and expression. I like to think that by not going to drama school I get much more flexibility over how I train. If I want to do more improv and less stage fighting for now, then I can, and if I want to pick up stage fighting later, that's fine too. I don't ever plan to stop learning.

Interview – Dimitra Barla

Dimitra Barla is a professional actress. She studied in Greece, London and LA and works in film, theatre and commercials. She started off acting in one-woman shows and has recently appeared in a significant feature film.

"Mindframe is important for getting the job. This is the only thing that is in your control. Don't put yourself down. You can think 'I'm never going to make it' but even if you don't get the part you meet people. There is always something to be gained. There is a casting director that keeps calling me back even though she hasn't cast me and this is an important step. There is a saying in LA – 'Book a room even if you don't book a job'. There is nothing that you can do about things that are out of your reach for example your hair colour might not match the other actor that has been cast or you might be the wrong height.

I think it is very important that you always do your own stuff whether it's a solo show, a web series, or just recording monologues on your phone. I actually do that from time to time (well, except I have a camera). I practice and film monologues and post them on my facebook page. I'm working on a script for a short film that I will then film and put out as a marketing tool for a feature.

Having a personal project keeps you creative and positive. It motivates you to work on the craft, to keep wanting to meet people and talk to people, to keep wanting to go to theatre and film festivals. And then the opportunity will come and you need to be ready for it. Opportunity doesn't really exist – you either build your career or you do a personal project. People who are out there have been through all those steps: you don't just push a button and get a lead in a feature. No one will trust you to do a feature if you haven't done short film. No-one will pay you in a short film until they see you can do it, until you have a showreel.

It's really important that you have a pool of people who support you: friends, family, colleagues. You can doubt yourself so much. All creative people should have a network of support.

It can sound a bit alternative to be positive, but to me it's really practical. Being positive means to wake up an hour earlier to do yoga, to calm down before I go to bed or to do a voice warmup for 45 minutes. It really is quite practical. Or doing an extra shift in my non-acting job so that I have the money for acting. Keeping involved is keeping positive. Also, have a plan of progress. I have a plan of where I want to go and I have a plan of how to get there. Somewhere to focus your energy and you can work towards that goal. Then things happen because you are concentrated. From the moment you have a goal you can really organise your life. Positive means being active and pro-active, not letting anxiety overrule you into inertia. Being positive is not pretending that everything is OK but doing all the work that you have to do.

I think theatre is for everyone. When I was young I knew that was the life I wanted to lead, but some people have the revelation later in their life. Sometimes people want to be involved and not give up their job or their lifestyle. But there is a difference if you do it as a professional. Your lifestyle choices will be different if it is your profession. You will think 'This is my clear priority. I will put all my energy to have the best artistic results for my profession. I have demands on myself to artistically progress.' – even if it is an unpaid project. Of course it is a goal to get paid, but that cannot be the priority. It's for everyone, it's healthy that people are involved in any kind of art.

It's unfortunate that it's so expensive to go to drama school because so many people can't go. If you work and do drama school at the same time you are very tired and you miss things. I had to work one year when I was at drama school and it was very hard. It's doable but it's very hard. You do get very tired and then you might give up. Drama schools are hard, very intensive. Eventually I stopped working when I was at drama school because I thought 'I just can't do it any more'. It's not rosy after drama school. You will have to balance bills and creativity; this will be your life for a while.

In London there are other things to do without attending drama school. There are classes and organised courses. What is good about drama school is that it gives you a curriculum. There is a longer goal so you can deepen your training but it's not the only way. There are so many shorter courses, say three months or so. So there are alternative training methods, which can be very good too. Sometimes drama school is a bit outside of reality; you get institutionalised. It's important to keep yourself updated with what's going on. Drama schools now create showreels for their students, (it didn't happen when I did it), but you're still not really ready after three years, you don't have the marketing tools.

My tips are 1. Watch films or go to theatre. 2. Always ask yourself why you want to do it. Seriously ask yourself. Why? Why? It's important that you define this why because it will support you and sustain you. 3. Keep training, either on your own or with other people but just keep doing it. 4. Have a personal project. 5. And finally, something that I learnt in LA. An agent said 'You are a business. The name of your business is Dimitra Barla. Your product is named Dimitra Barla. The president is Dimitra Barla. The CEO is Dimitra Barla. The people on your board are your agent etc, but you are a business and you need to market your product.' The sooner you get that in your mind, the better it's going to be."

STARTING OUT IN THE "INDUSTRY" – AUDITIONING AND CASTING SITES

One of the first small steps that I did on my journey towards becoming an actor was to ask everyone I knew for help. The world of acting is large with many tendrils going out into other areas of business and life. I met actors and ex-actors at my women in tech meetups, I got improv class recommendations from developers in my day job. It seemed that almost whenever I met someone new, they had a friend who had been there already or who had links in to the acting world in another way.

I started to hear a common story about how things worked:

1. You learn how to act. (Sounds so easy when you put it like that, right?)
2. You work for free to get experience, build a CV and create a showreel to show what you can do.
3. You get an agent to get better quality paid work.
4. You meet casting directors so that they ask your agent to ask you to audition.

I found getting on and taking classes to be a really easy and straightforward process. As I mentioned in the previous chapter, there are hundreds of good quality part-time classes in London, addressing a whole variety of acting skills (and even tangential skills such as how to keep working, how to keep your spirits up and how to manage your time).

But I was keen that as well as taking classes, I also started "working". I was very humble about my potential. I did not start out expecting to be cast in the West End or on TV. I knew that I would have to work for free, and I was fine with that.

Over the years I have heard many scare stories about things that will stop you from ever being considered for an acting role ever again. I heard my first when I was a child, taking classes with a local drama group. One of the boys had been cast in an advert (I have a vague recollection that it was for Fairy Liquid) and the older students and teachers were discussing what this meant for his career. It was universally agreed that acting in adverts was good for your career but acting as an extra in a film would be death to your future prospects and should never be done at any cost. Aside from "appearing in a dreadful movie", which has not impinged on any of the current Hollywood stars careers to go by the number of cheap (and extremely poor) movies that they appear in on their rise to the top, the other "death knell" for actors is appearing in AmDram.

I started my career unphased by this and I continue in the same vein. When most "professional" actors get paid little or nothing for their work, I find the stratifying off of some work as "amateur" to be rather meaningless. I do think that you should choose carefully who you work with, but this is based on individuals rather than on labels and titles.

I had a hope that amateur dramatics would be more open to people who did not have formal training, which it was, and also that it would be less competitive. Which it was not. Of the groups I subscribed to, one even had a pre-audition process so that you could only audition for a show if you had already proven yourself to be good enough in general (gulp!).

Auditioning

There are a very large number of amateur groups in London, all putting on regular shows, and so in no time at all I was receiving casting notices. I figured that I needed to get experience in the casting process, so I applied for everything that I thought I could be suitable for. The first audition that I did was for a show that I didn't know and can't remember, but I do remember that they sent us a piece from April de Angelis' The Positive Hour to audition from.

Waiting to go in, I had my first shock. I was sitting next to a lovely lady who worked as a PA and we got chatting. She showed me her CV, which she had brought in addition to the entry form we had to complete. I had left the question on the form "What experience do you have? (Continue on a separate sheet if needed.)" blank as I had nothing to use except the school pays I had done 20-odd years earlier. My new friend had BBC radio credits, other plays she had done and enough to fill a whole acting CV. This was the competition!

The audition itself went very well. I had learnt some basic acting concepts through my evening classes and did what I considered an adequate performance. I was momentarily destroyed when the director offered a much better textual interpretation than I had used, but was then reassured that it was only to see whether I could take direction. I was not too disheartened when I found out later that I did not get the part. After all, it was my first audition!

Having been trained in the value of feedback, I immediately asked what I could have done better. I received a short but positive reply that my performance had been fine, but that I just wasn't the right age for any of the parts (which did make sense as I'm rather "in between" if you want to have a play with two generations of adults).

My first audition may have gone well, but my experience went steadily downhill from there. My next was a little worse, then I had one with an American accent, which was outright poor. (My ego was salved only by the fact that I had luckily chosen to audition on a night when no-one else was available so only the director and producer saw my terrible accent.) Auditioning in a non-native accent went on a new list of "parts I would not be auditioning for".

My fourth audition added several more things to that list. It was also my worst audition ever™ and is in serious competition with the time a dentist did root canal work without adequate anaesthetic as the worst experience in my entire life. I kid you not.

I had decided that I would go out on a bit of a limb and audition for a musical. I was auditioning for the lead role, because of rule number one on "parts I do not audition for" – all other roles were asking for General American accent. The musical was a rather dated but slightly cute cross-dressing extravaganza called Victor/Victoria. The basic premise is that a singer, down on her luck in Paris, starts a new career as a female impersonator i.e. she starts pretending to be a man, so that she can make a living pretending to be a woman again. She is of course, very convincing.

She ends up dating a homophobic gangster, who although relieved that she has turned out to be a woman, can't cope with being seen with her in public dressed as a man. They reach a compromise (a rather unsatisfactory one for modern taste, I would say) that he will give up being a gangster as long as she, in return, gives up dressing as a man.

Victoria has some lovely songs, from the amazing Le Jazz Hot – her female impersonator show piece – to Living in the Shadows, a poignant song about having to pretend to be someone you're not. I was having singing lessons at the time and worked and worked on these songs. I practised my lines, and I wasn't worried about the dance part of the audition because leads don't dance so much, right?

Wro-o-ong. Turning up for a half day all round audition, we started with a dance audition. Everyone did the same audition, whichever role they were auditioning for or even if they were auditioning specifically to be a dancer. I found out later that the group has their own dance troupe who perform regularly.

I had done various jazz, ballet and tap classes when I was a child (20+ years previously) so I wasn't that phased by the set up and I assumed that it would "come back to me". The choreographer stands at the front, teaches you a line, and then you repeat it back.

Only it didn't come back to me. I suddenly realised that we were expected to learn this dance really, really quickly. I couldn't keep up at all. I started to feel acutely embarrassed. I went into that place where you start trying to pretend that you're invisible and hope everything will stop soon. It's harder to pretend to be invisible when you're 5'10". I was next to a lovely smiley lady, who noticed I looked a bit down and said, "It's all fun, isn't it?". As has been the case throughout my life when I am upset and trying to hide it, this small bit of kindness broke me. I started sobbing in the dance audition. If I was embarrassed before, well goodness me, I was a lot more embarrassed now. And, pragmatically, aware that crying probably wouldn't help me to get the role. I worked my way to the end of the dance section, including through a tap audition, where it turned out that everyone was practically a professional tap dancer too. The only good thing about a patronising (if heartfelt) "Thank you for trying" from the director, was that it signalled that there would be no further dancing.

I had time to break after the dance audition and I knew that I had to calm my nerves before I was called in to sing. I went outside and got some fresh air, got some water and did calming exercises. By the time I had finished I felt pretty pleased with myself. Despite the horror of the dance audition I no longer felt any nerves at all and I was ready to redeem myself. I was sure that dancing wouldn't be the key part of the audition for the lead role so I might still be able to salvage it.

I walked into the casting room. I had a choice of two songs, the upbeat Le Jazz Hot or the more sedate Living in the Shadows, which was nicely in my range. I was a bit worried because I hadn't practised with a proper accompanist, but I had practised a lot so I figured I would be OK.

I chose Living in the Shadows. The music started, I found my note and sang the first line. It ended on a long note. My voice was all over the place. It was shaking really badly. I couldn't even tell whether I was singing the right note. It seems that I had not banished my nerves, merely hidden them from myself. It was humiliating and painful.

As a final indignity, it turns out that the sides that I had assiduously learnt for the acting audition had been the wrong ones. I had to read for the acting part of the audition (rather than reciting my beautifully learnt lines) and I was completely thrown by needing to execute a stage punch that I had not been expecting. Knockout.

When I got home I could do nothing but sit on the sofa. For the whole rest of the day I felt as if I would never to be able to attempt anything in my life ever again. It was as if I was totally shell shocked.

At the time I felt as if it was my fault, that I was a bad actor and that would be the end of everything. I felt that this had been "the role" that I needed to get in order to start my career. I also just felt totally humiliated and exposed. I consoled myself by adding "singing" and "dancing" to the list of "things that I will never do in an audition again". This was a saving grace for me. It wasn't actually my acting that had failed. I had other things I could blame.

I was wrong though, about everything I felt after that audition. Bad auditions happen to every actor. Including auditions that are this bad, where you start to doubt yourself and your potential. If I had felt exposed on my acting, if someone had told me I was "the worst actor they had ever seen" (apparently Peter Jackson delivered this cutting critique to Jake Gyllenhaal when he auditioned for Lord of the Rings) maybe it would have knocked me out for even longer.

The good news is that the further out of your comfort zone you are, the more you are learning. I learnt two really important things from my worst audition ever. First that I had a great ability, that had stood me well through stressful work meetings and presentations – of hiding my nerves. I was great at gritting my teeth and bearing it. I realised that this was a terribly quality for an actor and that I would need to work hard on letting go of my nerves instead of damping them down.

Secondly I learnt that however bad you feel, you get over it. You live to fight another day. Like with the poorly anesthetised dental work, the painful memory of that audition (nearly two years ago!) has faded.

The reason that all actors find auditions challenging is that you are putting yourself up to be judged. In many walks of life you can build up your confidence while you build your expertise by "winning" at most things that you do. This way by the time you reach a task that you fail at, you have all the memories of the tasks that you completed to make you realise that the pattern is still an upward trend. Auditioning is a sport where you lose most of the time. Modern psychology tells us that we need five positive experiences to balance every one negative experience. No wonder we all find auditioning so tough.

Once you know that you will fail most auditions and that no-one can cope with constant rejection, there is only one solution to how to keep doing it. You need to find a way to stop auditions being a negative experience. The first thing is to see an audition as a process, as something that you are doing regardless of the outcome. This might sound crazy, but I've heard from many directors that the best actors that they see have been to ten auditions already that day and are not too emotionally invested in their particular audition.

I now fire off applications for roles without thinking twice about whether I will get them. If I get invited in to audition that is a nice bonus; if I feel I did well at an audition that is the best I can hope for. That is all that I have control over.

The second way to help detoxify auditions is to not take any rejection personally. When I first went to auditions I would routinely write off to get feedback. I wanted to know whether I had done OK or not. Investing this much into an audition is too much. It can be much easier to just see it as a matching system. Castings are often decided by factors that you have no control over.

Edmund Duff, an actor in London, told me about a time he went to audition for Kenneth Branagh. It turned out that by coincidence Edmund had recently bleached his hair and so had Sir Kenneth. The assistant director clocked it straight away and chipped in with an immediate "he's got hair like yours". To which Sir Kenneth shouted "OUT!". Confused and abashed Edmund had to leave the room. He didn't even get to audition. The result of that audition had nothing to do with his acting ability – how could it have?

Casting, especially for film and TV, often requires a very specific "look" whether this is to do with physical characteristics or things that might only get noticed at auditions, such as mannerisms or accent. It is more likely that it was something along these lines that was the reason that you were turned down. The quicker you can get to a place where you book, attend and forget auditions, and move on to the next one, the better.

Another tip that I have for when you are starting out is to view auditions as a practice to get good at auditions. Auditions are a separate skill to acting on stage or on a film shoot. Bad auditions are confirmation that you have what it takes to keep going when it gets tough.

Casting Sites

Like with everything else in the modern world, the internet is democratising acting. Twenty years ago if you didn't have an agent you would have to work extremely hard to find opportunities to practice your craft. Students were making films, but you would have to contact the film departments directly and hope that they kept you on file. Similarly with fringe theatres.

Nowadays there are hundreds of thousands of actors trying to find their own work, and work experience, via the internet. Correspondingly there are many fledgling production companies who are keen to take advantage of this vast pool of cheap resource for their projects.

This means that online casting sites are extremely popular and the barrier to entry is very low. You could set up a profile right now and start applying for roles. The flip side of a low barrier to entry is that the competition is fierce. Casting Call Pro, one of the most popular sites, proudly boast of having 58,000 actors on their site. This is great if you are casting for a short film. It makes for terrible odds of getting cast if you are an actor.

Still, terrible odds are not the same as no odds and if you are vigilant for new roles and responsive when people ask you to audition, you can start to build credits that then increase your chance of getting cast for the next role.

It is also important to know how casting is done. A first round of any casting, from the hundreds of applications that come in, is usually done by sorting on photo. As a director (or a casting director trying to find actors that the director will like) you are looking for people who come across in a certain way. If you have a vision of your lead as blonde and sharp-looking, you will filter applications to those whose photo matches this. In terms of getting through this first stage of casting your headshot photos are even more important than your showreel. No-one has time to watch a hundred three-minute video clips.

Given this, it is worth investing in professional headshots with a good headshot photographer. I was dubious of this when I first looked into acting, as I was warned a lot when I was younger about tricksters who would charge you a fortune for "model portfolio" shots that would not help you in any way to become a model. Acting headshots are different and professional actors pay hundreds of pounds a time to have them updated regularly. A good photographer will capture your personality in the shot, which is exactly what a casting director is looking for.

The advent of cheap digital cameras does mean that you don't need to invest in headshots straight away (even if you will need to do so eventually). Any photo that meets the brief – i.e. head and shoulders only, not too much makeup or dramatic expression, no background clutter – will be accepted, even if the site says "professional photos only". Just don't try to submit a photo taken at your mate's wedding, with your partner visibly cut off to the right.

Having a showreel is great, but remember that it will take time to accumulate enough footage to create one. You can pay for a showreel shooting, where a script and scenario is invented in order to film snippets for your showreel, but it usually works better (and is much more satisfying) to gradually build up from work you have done. Sites like Shooting People have a network of many editors who will cut your short film appearances into a showreel at very low cost. Unlike headshots, where it is worth investing, showreels can be done very cheaply (provided you are getting high quality footage from your work/work experience).

The golden child of all casting sites is Spotlight. Established in 1927, Spotlight charges actors to have a profile and also charges production companies to look for actors. You're guaranteed both high quality people and high quality roles to apply for. The only catch is that you must prove that you are a professional actor before Spotlight will take your money. That means graduating from an accredited drama school or having four professional credits. Spotlight is very particular about their professional credits. Short films and web series do not count. Only feature film, TV and theatre. Longer term you should aim to get onto Spotlight, but give it at least 12-24 months. Spotlight is a great credential site but without an agent, you are unlikely to have the chance to apply for great roles through the site. There's no rush.

It's clear to me that the big game, therefore, in using online casting sites is finding a way to change the odds. If you have a one in a thousand chance of being asked to audition, then you need to apply for one thousand roles before you can expect to get an audition. If you have a one in five chance of being cast from an audition, then you need to apply for five thousand roles before you can expect to be cast in one role. Even if you have become very efficient at applying (which might not work in your favour – I'll explain in a minute) and can do so in ten minutes, that's several months of applying for auditions non-stop 8 hours/day for 6 days/week. You can spend your time more wisely than this!

The best way is to find sites that have many people making films and fewer actors. Shooting People is a fantastic example of this. Set up as a community resource for people who want to work together to make films, Shooting People often has casting notices and has fewer actors registered than Casting Call Pro or Spotlight. Of course as more actors realise this, more are joining, so the odds are decreasing daily. Smaller film circles are constantly springing up. I joined Nick Hilton's London Film Collaborative early on in my career and worked on four short films as a result of connections made there. Always think about how to be part of a group where there are fewer actors. Even if there are also fewer films, you are still likely to have a better chance of getting involved.

It is also worth thinking carefully about how you will present yourself when you apply for roles online. You will face a constant quandary. You need to apply for as many roles as possible in order to get a chance of being interviewed. Yet, with such a wide selection of actors available, casting directors are looking for someone who is "different", someone who meets the brief more exactly.

Many sites will have a way for you to save a standard application. (Even if this facility is not available on the site, you can always store some text offline and cut and paste it in yourself.) But if you really want a role you may need to add some background knowledge or specify why you fit this particular role. For example "I am often cast as mid-30s professional women".

I recently applied for a role as Aileen Philby, the wife of the Soviet agent Kim. The director very kindly took some time out to reply to all applicants and explain how he was looking for in-depth knowledge of the character in order to cast. This was very kind of him and I replied to say so. However I declined to go and do the research. I didn't feel that a half-arsed Google would help me, when there are no doubt actors who also specialised in cold war history that I am competing with.

One of my favourite tips for applying for roles is to "fire and forget". When I first started applying I got really excited about every potential role, and started pencilling all the shoot dates into my calendar. This level of investment in each role meant that I had frequent, and extremely painful, disappointments. Now I apply and let it go. If I get an audition I do the same thing. I turn up, do my best, leave, and forget about it. (OK, in reality I try to forget about it but keep wondering, especially if I feel the audition went well. But I'm no longer waiting expectantly for the call. The industry just doesn't work that way.)

Interview – Alison Goldie

Alison Goldie is (and in no particular order) an actor, a director, a facilitator, a life-coach and the writer of The Improv Book: Improvisation for Theatre, Comedy, Education, and Life (Oberon). She started out in stand-up and improvisation, worked on mainstream TV and radio and then formed a theatre company and toured internationally. Alison's website is www.alisongoldie.com.

"A career in the arts is not linear. There is no ladder to climb – it goes up and down. One great highlight of my career was touring the world with The Weird Sisters theatre company – myself, Kath Burlinson and a technician. We went to any country with enough English to understand us, and we were performing every night. There was loads of travel – I love travel, meeting people and performing.

Most of my TV career was in the 90s. I got job as TV presenter after doing sketch acting and comedy journalism on various channels. Suddenly out of the blue, because I had sent a video of myself presenting a made-up item to the BBC, I got an offer to be a presenter on BBC 2's The Travel Show. It was a very exciting job to get, but ended up being a mixed blessing. The travelling was brilliant, but some of the politics were not so brilliant. I couldn't be at all self-determining. I was told what to say, what to wear, what to look like – 'stick the blonde in front of the camera and make her look cute in a wholesomely sexy way'. I was told to repress aspects of myself. I was employed because I was an improviser and then never allowed to improvise. In the end I realised that presenting was straight-jacketing. I just wasn't very "biddable". I stopped trying to get TV work and instead put on a play with my friend for our own self-gratification. And thus I began six and a half years of travelling around the world. My agent dropped me because I was never in the UK, but I was having a ball!

The Weird Sisters started in England and did a few nights at a fringe theatre in London that belonged to The Hackney Empire. Roland and Clare Muldoon who used to run the Empire had given us cabaret work as The Wild Girls in the 80's then they gave us a small theatre to use for free as The Weird Sisters because they loved us. (Tip: make sure you ask everyone you've ever known for favours.) We did pub theatre in the UK and then applied for festivals around the world. We would pay our festival registration fee and keep the box office receipts. A Dutch producer saw one of our shows at the Edinburgh Fringe and said "I would like to book this show for a 36-date Dutch tour". That was a good break, and then we did two more Dutch tours in successive years. We put all our profits back into the company. We took enough to live on but spent everything else on touring, for example, covering the costs to go to Adelaide Fringe Festival where we beat five hundred entrants to win The Grand Prize for our show 'Loveplay' in 2000.

I've never earned much money, and it's a lot harder to earn a living as an actor or comedian nowadays. When I started in comedy, it was just post The Comic Strip, and comedy was really on the rise. There was a lot of variety, not just stand-up. We got paid cash after the gig and I could live on 2 or 3 gigs a week and pay London rent. And then I could spend the rest of my time writing material for the gigs. Nowadays you need to do unpaid guest spots over and over again to even have a chance of getting a paid comedy gig.

It helps not to be materialistic – you'll need that as a quality if you want to be a performer. If you're just doing it for the money, it will sap your will. At the same time, it's really important to know your own value and have your threshold, decide what your bottom line is. It's so easy to work for no money at all and then you might start hating yourself.

One unfairness in the industry is that casting directors and agents are reluctant to look at someone who hasn't been to drama school. As a director, when I cast directly from Spotlight; I always leave a few slots for rogue people doing it on their own because I'm an equal opps employer. But with drama school graduates, it is fair to say you are more likely to find someone of quality, because they will have had thorough training.

It's not too late to go to drama school if you are retraining later in life. You'd have to be a bit tough to cope with being the oldest person in the class. However, I met a 60-year-old lady recently who only went to drama school a few years ago and she's very happy about it. She wanted to do it all her life and now it's her chance. She looks in her 60s and she's getting great 60-year-old women roles. It might not be well paid, but for her it can be a nice, occasionally paid hobby. She needed to go to drama school to get the confidence and hone her skills, but you might be able to get that from evening classes. You can find other ways to get training and practice if you're not able to go to drama school, and you're determined enough.

I had a phase of being with a co-op agency and getting put up for endless commercials. That's a year I won't get back. I would rather write and put on a show in a church hall than audition for endless commercials. I hate people looking at me like I'm worthless, like I'm on a conveyor belt. A lot of my work has been about keeping my dignity. Commercials are not bloody art! If you can call yourself an artist, if you can say 'I'm doing this because I have a yearning to express myself artistically' that is the only valid reason for doing it."

DOING IT YOURSELF

The traditional industry journey is all about getting approval from other people. At each stage of your career there are gatekeepers. If you want to go to drama school, you will be auditioned before you are accepted. To be able to apply for roles yourself via Spotlight, you must prove that you have acting credentials. Some places where you can take courses, such as The Actors Centre, require you to be (and to prove that you are) a "professional actor" before you can study with them.

Then in order to get any "serious" roles, for example small parts on TV series, you need to be registered with an agent. You see, there are so many actors that TV production companies don't want to put out a general call to all actors. They don't have time to sift through all the replies that they will receive. So instead they send their roles only to trusted agents, who select from their stable of actors and send people who match the role. This way the production company knows that the actor will be a match for the role and that they can act.

So once you have proved yourself to acting training providers and online casting sites you must prove yourself to agents, which is a much harder step. But even then it's not over! Agents often have hundreds of actors on their books and while (good) agents will do their best for each actor, they don't have time to market each one individually. The final stage is that you must go and prove yourself individually to casting directors, so that when your agent sends them your photo and showreel they will remember you fondly and cast you.

And of course, the concomitant of all this is that you will be rejected over and over and over and over. This constant battle for other people's approval one of the things that is so dispiriting and makes people quit acting. Whatever we do, however good it is, the need to chase approval from other people can make it all taste of ashes.

The need to get approval from others means that we take the wrong mindset to our classes. Instead of going with our own learning agenda, we want the teacher to approve of us. I have felt a big difference when I go to a class simply to learn. I learn much more and in a much more enjoyable way when I can let go of whether the teacher (or the other students!) think I am good.

For the first six months of my acting career, I did not perform in a single show. I had taken a lot of advice (which I've included in the Industry chapter above) and I was following it. I was applying for all roles that I was a fit for, and I was auditioning for one or two a month. But I was getting cast in nothing.

I had found so many people willing to help me. Contrary to how it can feel sometimes, when you are starting out everyone wants you to succeed. If you ask for help, people will give it, more often than not.

I have been a member of an organisation called Women in Film and TV for several years (I joined as a presenter). They were hosting a talk and Q&A with an American coach called Amelie Mettenheimer. She describes herself as an "A-ha! Moment Creator" and what really attracted me to her was that she advises actors on how to move across to LA. (Moving to LA was part of my original vision for my perfect life as an actor.)

There was only one problem. I had a work engagement on the evening of her talk that I absolutely could not move. I was just about to sigh and delete the email, when I had an inspiration. I looked up her contact details from her website and dropped her an email. Would she be able to answer a few questions by email for me?

I am used to people helping, but Amelie's answer blew me away. "Don't be silly," she replied, "I can do better than that. How about thirty minutes free coaching by phone?" I was really excited by this. Lots of actors have coaches to help not just with acting technique but also with their career. Coaches are expensive, and it is hard to decide to invest this money when you are starting out. A free session was an amazing opportunity!

I had to wait a few weeks for an available slot with Amelie. I had my questions lined up. They were mostly about getting an agent – whether I should and how I should go about it if so? (This was to become a recurring theme in my career). Amelie surprised me by side-stepping that question and immediately turning to fundamentals. "How did I know I wanted to be an actor?" I explained about the Artist's Way. "Fine", she said, but had I ever been on stage? Did I know that I enjoyed acting itself?

I was rather thrown by this question. I had been so sure that I was on the right path to acting. By answering the question of why I wanted to be an actor with "A magic book told me to" (I still love giving this answer), I had been quite well protected from difficult follow up questions. I explained rather sheepishly that I was very sure I wanted to be an actor, but that no I had not been on stage since I was at school. I further explained that this was not my fault, that I was applying for all the roles that I could but that no-one would cast me.

"Nonsense!" said Amelie Mettenheimer. "You must devise a one-woman show and put yourself on the stage. Only then will you know whether you want to be an actor or not". Wow! A real a-ha moment.

I had no idea where to start, but my brief chat with Amelie had somehow convinced my inner goal setter that it could be achieved. Over the next few days I mused on what I could do a one-woman show about. I had heard that everyone can make a one-person show about some aspect of their life. Yet I felt that my life was nowhere near interesting enough to entertain people for 60 minutes.

I find that when I have a problem that I can't find the answer to with my conscious brain, ideas can often come to me if I let it swish around in my unconscious. And sure enough, after failing to find anything in my life that I could talk about, I remembered that my friend Tracey Sinclair had written an amazing series of novels, Dark Dates, about a young woman who started a dating agency to match vampires with humans. That would be a fun idea.

I emailed Tracey to see what she thought of this idea. I still had no idea how to go from Tracey's books to a script, but that didn't faze Tracey. She agreed (YES!) to let me use her material for a show and offered to knock up a first draft of a script based on the main storyline of her first novel (DOUBLE YES!). We had an idea that we could set the show as if I were Cassandra Bick (Tracey's lead character) hosting a speed dating event for vampires, and that I would end up explaining about some things that had been happening to me i.e. tell the story from Tracey's first Dark Dates book.

It was when I had read the Artist's Way six months earlier that I had come across the concept of synchronicity, which is best summed up by the aphorisms that Julia Cameron offers in the book. "Leap and the net will appear." "Take one step towards the universe, and the universe takes ten steps towards you." The idea is that if you put yourself and an idea "out there", the pieces that are missing will come to you.

I had just joined the Actors Centre in London to take part in their fantastic Script to Screen course (where I took part in my first short film), and the second piece of my puzzle was delivered to me via their email newsletter. It turns out that every year in February-March, the Actors Centre run a festival of solo performance. As a member I could submit a show. How perfect!

I looked up on the internet how to write a proposal, and tried to work out my target audience, vision for the show and other such tempting facts to encourage the Actors Centre theatre – The Tristan Bates Theatre – to commission it. I had no idea how many applications they received and hence how likely I was to get a place, but I did! I was offered a single night on 23rd February 2015 at 7pm with a show to immediately follow on from mine.

With that booked, I now knew that the show had to go ahead. I had some material but I had no idea how to turn it into an engaging performance. I knew what I was missing, and that was a director. I was new to the acting world and didn't have any contacts. How could I find a director? Could I advertise for one? What if they weren't any good? What if they didn't want to work with a complete beginner?

In order to find a director I used a tried and trusted method that has helped me throughout my acting career. I asked for help. I had just started the Script to Screen course, so I asked the other actors if they knew anyone. And I was absolutely amazed by the first answer that I got. Fellow actor Cindy Armbruster said that she had a friend who was a director and who specialised in one woman performances! Amazing! Cindy said that she would ask her friend, Peta Lily if she might be interested. I was worried that a well-established director and performer like Peta wouldn't want to work with a complete newbie like me so I kept looking.

I think it is worth a little digression here on how people in the acting world react to complete beginners. The stereotype is that they will first try to establish whether you have any talent, then either cruelly dismiss you (if you have none) or shout at you while they help you to put on a play (if you are totally amazing). Sadly this approach is all too common in the world of acting (and indeed in many other professions!). It seems that many people forget what things were like for them when they were starting out, or perhaps they were treated this way and feel that it is the only way to go. There are many people in the acting world who seem to go out of their way to make you feel bad. These include directors and other actors, and sometimes even class tutors – whose role should be to encourage you and help you to perform at your best!

There are different views on what makes the best learning environment for people. Having learnt about working with people in my day job, I have developed very strong views. Positive feedback is essential. Constructive feedback is great, but only if the person you are feeding back to has enough confidence (given to them by positive feedback!) to be able to take on board what you are saying. There is a suggested ratio that you should use in giving positive:negative feedback of 5:1. That means that you cannot point out something that someone is doing wrong until you have found five things that they are doing right.

I learnt, first when I did finally work with Peta Lily, and also increasingly throughout my career that there are (thankfully!) people in the acting world who understand this. It is very easy to end up in a class where you feel like you are just taking constant abuse. You don't need to do this. Hold out and find people that you enjoy working with. It is the only way that you will learn and grow, and retain enough joy in the process of acting to keep going. It's hard when you are starting out if you feel like you are missing an opportunity, but it is not necessary to work with people who make you feel like crap. I've now worked with many people who are open and encouraging to beginners including (but not limited to) Peta Lily, my current coach Jeremy Stockwell, Nick Cohen the great director that I worked with on the Actors Centre script to screen course and London Actors Workshop tutor Jon Sigwick. Spend your time searching out the people who have enough decency to make you feel good about yourself. They are out there!

Peta Lily first asked that we do an initial "chemistry session" together. I was terrified! I felt that this was a way for her to test out "how good" I was and decide whether I was good enough to be worth her time. I felt that the whole success of my project would rest on this one interaction. In a way I was right, but I was also wrong. I've come across chemistry sessions again when working with other performers. Chemistry sessions are not about testing how good you are but whether the you are able to work well together. An actor can be fantastically skilled, but if for some reason they do not resonate with the way that the director wants to work then the relationship will fail.

I needn't have worried though, as Peta was so lovely and so easy to work with I regularly forgot that I felt I was being tested and just got on with having fun. We did some amazing exercises. I'm still at the stage in my career where I find a new warm up exercise exciting! We also did some work where I took on each of the characters in the book and improvised as them, which gave some deeper insight into the story and the character interactions.

I had such a great time that I wasn't surprised at all when Peta said that she would be happy to continue working with me. It all felt extremely natural. I've learnt that this is a good sign. If you ever feel like you are trying to force something – a role, a relationship, a job – to work then often it means that it isn't the right fit. Peta Lily and me and Tracey Sinclair's fantastic vampire story were a great fit.

I would love to be able to explain about the creative process so that you can copy it and make your own show, but I was definitely led by Peta in this creation. So a good tip if you are starting out and unsure how to create a show is to find someone else to work with. If you are lucky enough to be able to find a professional director that you work well with (and you are able to afford their time!) that is a great way to do it. There are also many courses now that will help you to work an idea into a show, or even to come up with the idea in the first place. The Actors Centre has a great range of courses for devising material, and Colin Watkeys runs a company called Solo Theatre and puts on the Solo Theatre Festival annually. He runs fabulous courses that will help you to find characters and material in the most unexpected of places.

I was enthusiastic about the show that Peta, Tracey and I had created and determined for it to be a success. I rallied round everyone I knew through my various walks of life and managed to fill the sixty-seater theatre. (A note on organising a production: marketing and selling tickets is one of the most difficult parts of producing a show. In the event I realised what a good job it was that I had been so gung-ho in getting my friends to come along as I had not a single walk-in from the street or through the advertising of the theatre. Everyone who was in the audience I knew personally.)

Doing a first show for one night only was a big challenge. I had no way to tell whether my nerve would fail in a performance environment rather than a rehearsal one. I had only been able to access the performance space on the day itself for the technical rehearsal (this can be quite usual) so I didn't know whether that would throw me. Would I find I had left some of my props in the wrong place and they would not be there when I went to use them? Would I forget my lines?

In the event I was really pleased with the show. It was the best performance I had done to date, the audience laughed and I got many kind comments including a lovely review written up in A Younger Theatre.

I had previously done quite a bit of public speaking and so I was very familiar with that sheer panic feeling in the stomach when your performance is slipping out of your grasp and you feel a desperate need to rein it back in. Luckily I didn't feel like that in my first performance! (I credit Peta's relaxation techniques that we did just before the show.) Although not panicked, I was nervous and it manifested itself as time passing really quickly while I was on stage. Although I didn't forget my lines I felt at several points that I must have missed a whole section because I seemed to have suddenly jumped ahead and couldn't remember whether I had done that bit or not.

This is the real training that you get from performing. You need to perform through the various stages of nerves, and crises of confidence, and stiffness and panic and you need to come out the other side so that you can face down the next performance challenge. I've now been through many stages of performance impairing emotions and I'm sure I have plenty more to go!

Putting on my show was a big fat training success. And it was incredible to learn that I could do it on my own. I had gone from being an actor who couldn't get cast in an amateur production to being someone performing in a one-woman show ("ooh, you're so brave, I could never do a show on my own" – was a frequent comment from other actors). It changed the way that other people saw me and the way that I saw myself.

Most of all, it encouraged me to put on another show, and then another. In August 2015 Julie-Ann Nye and I put on Chris Lee's Shallow Slumber at the Map Studio Café in Camden. I met Julie at one of the very first auditions that I did (she got a call back, I didn't), which was a great sign that nothing you do is ever wasted, even if it doesn't work out quite how you were intending.

Julie had been in a similar position to me, working in a day job and wishing she was acting instead. She took a bigger jump that me and quit her job to go back to drama school. She had just graduated when I met her and so, like me, is kicking off her professional career. She had studied a fantastic play called Shallow Slumber while studying at The Bridge, a theatre training school in North London. The play is about the relationship between a young mother and her social worker – the cast is two women.

Julie had a leap of intuition and suggested that we could do this play together. She had played the social worker when she previously studied and she was keen to get her teeth into the darker role of Dawn, the young mother. With my "professional 30-something woman" look, I would work well for Moira the social worker. Having produced Dark Dates, I found it much easier to co-produce Shallow Slumber with Julie. I knew what all the moving parts were and most of all, I knew it could be done, if you just took it one step at a time.

After Shallow Slumber, I received another email from the Tristan Bates Theatre. Would I like to propose a show for their members' week in December? After my great success working previously with Tracey Sinclair I asked her for permission to stage her debut play Bystanders, first aired in 2012 at Baron's Court Theatre.

Tracey agreed and I wrote and sent off a proposal. I based the format on the one that I had used for Dark Dates, as that had clearly worked well! I was pleased when I got a response back offering me one night. If I had thought longer and harder about the format of the week, and the fact that the Tristan Bates would need to fit a lot of shows in in a single week, I probably would have realised that I was most likely to be offered a single night performance. I hadn't thought this through, however, and now I had some sudden doubts. I knew that putting on a show involved a large amount of time and expense. Was it worth it for just a one night show?

I can't remember exactly what process I went through, but I decided to take the plunge. I suspect my reasoning went something like "You don't have so many offers lined up that you can afford to be picky, my girl". I was worried though – would I regret this decision later?

I put this to one side and got on with the job at hand. Next, I needed to get a director on board. I had very much enjoyed working with Peta Lily, and I wanted to get some experience with another director to see how their approach was different (or similar!). I had been working with Jeremy Stockwell as a private coach (and I strongly recommend him if you are looking for one!) and I was intrigued to see how his approach would map on to directing, rather than coaching.

Jeremy agreed and suggested that he look for cast members from his contacts. Brilliant! We were now set, for a one night show. Then my project had a moment of synchronicity that turned it from an OK project to a perfect one. When was the show on again? Jeremy said. Would I also be interested in a one week run at the White Bear Theatre in Kennington? The artistic director Michael Kingsbury had recently been in touch with Jeremy to ask if he knew any shows that could fill a slot.

So by taking a leap of faith and committing to a single night performance, I ended up with a one week run. If I had turned down the offer from the Tristan Bates I would have turned down a single night but by accepting I accepted a decent run that would pay off all the hard work that we would need to do. I felt that this showed me an important lesson about life. You never know where opportunities are going to take you.

Having just completed the last performance of Bystanders eleven days ago at the time of writing this chapter, I have already started planning a new show for next year with Jeremy. Julie has also been in touch about staging an even darker play than Shallow Slumber. Producing plays is now a thing I do and I love it. It's fabulous to bring into being something that didn't exist before and to create opportunities for other people to work and perform. So many actors are not working.

Sometimes if you make your own productions you can worry that you are a fraud. When I was telling people that I was doing a one-woman show at the Tristan Bates, I often worried that it didn't count because I had cast myself. I didn't have the seal of approval of having been selected by an external director.

Having reflected on this a lot, a think that this is a fear driven by my ego. I wanted to be part of a production in order to gain experience and improve my acting. It was a brilliant success for that. Wouldn't it be a shame if I passed up on that opportunity because of my ego?

Another great reason to put on your own performances is that work generates work. It's great when you're asked at a casting what you were last doing to be able to name a show and talk about your experiences. They don't ask you this to catch you out, just to make conversation, and it's great to have something to talk about.

Many actors who start writing, producing or directing, find that they have another talent and that they enjoy their new role as much or more than acting. We forget that people are multi-dimensional and that we can have many interests and abilities. Being a director doesn't mean that you're not also an actor.

I've just started producing my first short film, which is a whole different game from producing theatre. Whereas in theatre there are many ways to find cheap venues, if you think outside of the box, and many of the jobs that are needed can be picked up quite quickly and done yourself, film is a whole new ball game. To make a film you need expensive equipment and technical skills.

You can start out by making a film on your phone or a cheap camera, but this is not necessarily the easy option. When you are limited in your equipment you need to be even more skilled to make a great film. Most films are made by really large teams of people and this is one of the main costs in making a film.

Our film is succeeding because of an excess of synchronicity, as described by Julia Cameron in the Artists Way. I met the scriptwriter Chris Brown at a networking event and casually asked if he had any short film scripts lying around. I only found out later that he had won awards for his previous shorts and for his debut feature film, which is in development. The director, Marianna Dean, advertised on Shooting People that she was looking for scripts to direct, and that was how we met.

Since then we met a stills photographer who was looking for experience, I remembered that I'd done an audition for a guy who is a great poster designer, we found a second producer and he knew a fabulous art director. We have got an amazing cast and we just need to book a crew once we have confirmed production dates. It's been my best experience of synchronicity yet!

Doing it yourself doesn't mean doing it on your own. You need to be the instigator and the overall driver behind the project but you'll also need to find other people to collaborate with (as I hope my examples show!). I've made some great friends and fantastic industry contacts through getting out there and making things. I hope you do too.

Interview – Keif Gwinn

Keif Gwinn is a startup entrepreneur, a standup comedian, an actor and a filmmaker.

"I decided to become an actor because it seemed like fun. I enjoyed school plays as a child – I was The Minotaur with a papier-mâché headset with macramé mounting and big horns. I was so into it that I spent several lunch breaks practising the fight scene choreography – it was the first time I was interested enough in something at school to do it off my own bat. I stopped when I went to High School; I dropped out of school and got a job. IT and computing was my passion for ten years or so and then I thought 'What else is there in life?', so I got into standup and then back into acting.

When I started getting into it, I was more interested in storytelling and producing i.e. writing and directing. For a friend's birthday we went to the comedy store. We met Greg Davies at the bar. He had mentioned in his act about previously being a teacher so we asked how he changed over. He said he just went on a course with Logan Murray. So I did a beginners course with Logan that included stage presence and standing up in front of people and then I realised that performing was kind of fun. The character work that we were doing was my way back into that kind of performing. I started writing – initially standup and then other stories.

Since then I have mostly appeared in my own stuff. I have acted in only one other piece that wasn't my own. To make your own stuff you just come up with a story and get some people together. Have a story that you want to tell. An example is the team we put together to make Lilies in Winter for the 48 hour Sci-fi competition. I had me and Phill (we collaborated on a lot of projects together) who could direct and DOP between us, Monique who we'd worked with before, and we met Zoe who had a location. We had equipment and the competition created our story.

When we were casting for our film 'Saturday' we had ten roles and six hundred applicants. We hired a casting director who filtered them to ten people per role and we interviewed 5-8 people per character. That was really interesting seeing actor after actor. I learnt that it's not just about their performance – it's very important to find people who are easy to chat with. We had someone who did an excellent audition and had a great CV but he was a bit odd. We took a chance on him and he was the worst person in the world to work with. He didn't attend rehearsals, he showed up late on the day, didn't know his lines. Being a decent human being who is easy to work with and flexible and accommodating can really work in your favour.

I acted in 'Saturday' very basically. By making things you get a 1:1 chance to act rather than 1:100 chance. We also cast people just by them being around when we need them. Being available is 90% of the job. Making yourself available gets you extra kudos.

Being asked to perform for the first time was nice. I was invited to come and join a short film about a Scottish fiver. It was a bunch of improvisers who'd been to Edinburgh and knew the pain of coming back and never being able to spend Scottish money. The story ends with them taking it to Scotland but no-one will take it there either. The team knew me from improvisation classes.

My advice is to try, act as many times as you can. Improvisation is great for trying out lots of different characters. It doesn't have to be wacky, but once a world's been created, it's best to be the most believable person in that world, which is excellent practice. The group is their own audience and you get to play and play and play. If you sit around waiting for a script, you'll never get around to being as many things as you need to be in order to be as realistic as possible. Finding the emotional reality of who these people are leads to better acting.

Is it a good career? No. It's a terrible career. It's almost impossible to get paid, and when you do get paid who don't know where the next job is coming from, for reasons that are entirely not your own fault. It's still a lot of fun. Absolutely explore it and do it if you have the time and the money backed up somewhere else. A couple of hours a week practise in improvising is great and you might get three short films a year. The alternative to spending 4-5 years in drama school and getting an agent is to grind your way up on the sidelines. Be prepared to fail, something I learnt from improv. Having a burning passion can be a bad thing because then when you get rejected it really hurts. Whereas if you just have fun – you can just brush things off."

NETWORKING

When I went through my list of what I could bring to an acting career from my previous life experiences, one thing that really stood out for me is networking. It's interesting because networking is something that everyone could easily do, so it's not that unique. On the other hand, most people I meet have an absolute horror of networking so I do feel that simply by understanding what networking is, that you can do it while being yourself and that it's not about taking advantage of other people, I do have a useful skill.

There are many books available on networking. In fact, I wrote one myself – *Networking Know-How* (also published by Urbane Publications) was the book that I wrote before this one. I love introducing people to networking because I am so passionate about it, and it breaks my heart when I see people missing out because they misunderstand.

Myths of networking

The following are my top five networking myths. I find that these have become a kind of self-perpetuating networking nightmare.

When you go networking you will meet loads of people who act like this. People who talk about themselves, big up what they have done previously and then ditch you when a prolific director turns up. These people will make you have a miserable time when you are networking. You then feel even worse when you reflect on the fact that networking is essential for your career and now you realise you must become one of these people in order to do it. So you force yourself to go out, be a fake you, try to impress people and have a miserable time. And so the cycle continues.

It doesn't need to be this way! Here are my top five misconceptions of networking that I hate. They make networking awkward, selfish and insincere. The rules for good networking are simple: be yourself, be nice and have fun.

Myth 1: Networking is all about sales.

Lots of people discover networking when they want something. They need a new job, or they are looking for someone to buy something from them. This is a dreadful time to be networking. Every person that you connect with will assume that you are only doing it to try and get something from them. As you will know from your own experiences that is a dreadful way to feel. If people you are speaking to think that you are just after something from them it will be impossible to make a real connection.

Making real connections is what networking is all about. It's about meeting the people that you genuinely enjoy spending time with. And if you network for long enough, and are picky enough about who you want to talk to, there are loads of brilliant networkers out there who know how to do it properly! So when you find that a networking event is full of people who just want to get something from you, keep looking until you find the genuine people who are interested in you and would like to have a genuine conversation.

Myth 2: You must pretend to be more successful, talented and charismatic than you are.

Many people get given a recommendation to be "the best version of themselves" when they go networking. And who wouldn't want to be that? But it's all too easy to interpret this instruction as an excuse to try to be someone that you're not. This might work in the short term, but in the long term it will do you no good whatsoever.

Remember, if networking is about making genuine connections, you can only do that by being yourself. Even if you put up a very convincing show of being someone else, you won't have a real connection with the person that you meet. You won't be able to relax and enjoy yourself. It's also very unlikely that the other person will warm to you. You must have felt this yourself when meeting people, you often get a slightly uncomfortable feeling whenever someone is trying too hard or projecting a surface gloss of fake personality.

Be you. You yourself are enough, whatever background, credits and experiences you have. You have nothing to prove to other people and no need to try and make yourself sound bigger than you are.

A great tip for networking is to focus on the other person rather than yourself. If you are feeling nervous in a room full of other people, it can be really helpful to focus on the fact that everyone else is feeling nervous. Yes, even those people who are talking very loudly and putting on a front. People only do that when they feel insecure.

Rather than leading with some examples of how you are fabulous and should be cast in their next film, ask questions about the other person. Take a genuine interest in their projects and hobbies. Try to find an area of common interest. Do you both come from the same part of the world? Or have an interest in the same type of films? If you can find something that you both love talking about, you'll soon be having loads of fun and completely forget that you are networking. You'll make a genuine friend who will want to stay in touch.

Myth 3: Networking is about having a pitch and pitching at as many people as possible.

One of the saddest conversations that I recently had about networking was at a private members' club with a guest, Sean. He said that he had recently been on a networking training course and he hadn't realised he had been doing networking so wrong. "I'd thought it was all about just keeping in touch with great people," he said with a glance at his friend Willson who had brought him along, "but the course tells me that's not it at all."

Sean had just been told that he needed a pitch, that he needed to plan who to talk to and he needed to start strategising to talk to the important people who could help him. In effect, he was being told to pretend to be someone else and ditch his friends. This was on a professional networking training course! No wonder networking gets such a bad name.

There is a use for a "pitch" in networking, although "pitch" is just a term for knowing what you will say to introduce yourself if someone asks you who you are. "I'm an actor and an accountant" would be a simple straightforward answer to the question if you also wanted to include your day job in your description of yourself. Your pitch can be context-dependent though. If you are at a film or acting event, an even shorter description of "I'm an actor" would also suffice. People want to know who you are in relation to the context that you are in. You do not need to recite your resume.

What you 100% do not need is some kind of sanitised five-minute pitch that lists your career highlights and credits and where you talk about what you could bring to someone's film. No one needs that. Wait until you are at an event and someone introduces themselves to you in this way and you'll know what I mean.

Your three goals at a networking event are to be yourself, be nice and have fun. You should introduce yourself in a way that fits with these goals. "I'm an actor" does the job perfectly. You could add "I've recently acted in the short film Symptoms and a new play Bystanders at the White Bear Theatre" but it's not really necessary. Most people love talking about what actors have been in, so you will almost definitely be asked as a follow up question what you have been doing recently.

I mentioned that a great strategy is to ask other people questions. This is always better than talking about yourself. So rather than listing out your best qualities for five minutes, try to find out what the person you are speaking with would have said if they had done that. You will be constantly amazed. If you take a genuine interest in the people that you are meeting you will start to discover that learning about them is much more fun that blowing your own trumpet.

And if you really want to know what networking is "all about", it's this. Networking is about helping other people. Good networking, that is. I mentioned before that you should be trying to make genuine connections and helping other people is a brilliant way to do that. Of course, it's important that you help them the right amount. We're not talking about changing all your plans so that you can work behind the scenes on their theatre show for free.

Adam Grant in his networking book Give and Take, suggests that doing something for someone else that takes about five minutes of your time is the right size to make your help. Common ways to help someone this much include sharing knowledge and making connections. Sharing knowledge could mean recommending someone to a great course that you have just been on, or sharing a great book on technique.

Making connections is where the real magic happens. Is someone desperate to meet a director that you know? Or are they looking for a helpful agent who could give them some advice? The great thing about connections is that they work both ways. By hooking people up with other people that might want to work with them, you actually help two people at the same time. And your five minutes of helping can end up being much more powerful than hours of work.

Myth 4: You must make sure you talk to the most important person in the room.

Networking is an amazing way to get to meet people, especially people that you wouldn't usually meet through any other channels. It's easy to jump to the wrong conclusion from this premise. I can see how you might think that this is a directive to run towards the most important or influential people in a room, for example making a beeline for directors and casting agents and leaving lowly fellow actors and technicians in your wake.

This is not what it means and what I have just described is a horrible way to do networking. The simple reason that this is not good networking is that is breaks several of the key principles. Actually, I think it often breaks all of them. You are not being nice and I doubt you are being yourself or having fun. It's not possible to make genuine connections this way. How can you when you are talking to people merely because of their title and not who they really are?

Networking done properly works because everyone is trying to help everyone else. It's like that rather sickly parable that was often told in school assemblies. The one about chopsticks. If you don't know it, it goes like this.

A man dies and goes to the pearly gates. St. Peter asks him if there's anything he wants before he enters heaven, and the man says he'd like to see hell. So St. Peter takes him down to hell. Hell is a room full of miserable, starving people with a huge banquet table in the middle filled with delicious-looking food. The man asks St. Peter, "Why is THIS hell?" St. Peter replies, "Because the people can only eat the food with 11-foot chopsticks." The man looks around and sees that it's true – everyone is picking up food desperately, but they cannot bring it round and into their mouths. The man then says he's ready to go to heaven, and St. Peter takes him up to a similar room. There is the same huge banquet table in the middle filled with delicious food and the same 11-foot chopsticks. Nothing appears to be different. The man asks St. Peter why this is different from hell, and St. Peter replies, "Here in heaven we all feed each other."

The idea is that the main benefit from networking is not from directly meeting the people that can help you. It's from building a helping network with other like-minded people, who then think of you when they are meeting people who might be a good connection for you. Or to put it another way, it's not your first degree connections that are important in and of themselves, it's the second degree connections that they are able to introduce you to that matters.

This explains why networking by being nice and by focussing on people with the right attitude rather than the fancy title works. The quality and number of someone's connections is not related to their job, but instead to how they go about meeting and staying in touch with people.

Another myth is that you should be giving your card out to every person in the room. First time networkers often feel panicked that they haven't met enough people at an event. What if the amazing networker was over there, and you didn't get around to meeting them? Relax. Networking is a long-term game. The real benefits from making great and long lasting connections are likely to come to you in one, two, five years' time, or maybe even longer. You don't need to meet everyone right now.

I have a rule that if you make one great connection at an event, that is enough. Someone that you really click with and enjoy talking to. If you achieve that, don't worry about speaking with everyone. If the connection is meant to be, a chance for it will come around again.

Myth 5: Networking is about politely smiling and nodding while secretly wishing you were somewhere else.

We have a tendency in our control-obsessed culture to make things better by working on them. If you're not happy, get an app with exercises to make sure that you get happier. If you need relaxation, do a class. If you want to find love work on sorting yourself out first.

So if you have decided you want to get better at networking, I imagine that one of the first thing you will do is to try to work out how you can work at it and make it better. Lots of people also think that "working" is the opposite of "having fun". It must be, right? Work is something you are doing to achieve another goal (often, but not always, that goal is getting paid) whereas fun is something that you do just for the sake of it.

If you've ever had a job you enjoyed (sadly so many people don't!), then you'll know that in general it's easier to do most work better if it's also fun. That was definitely a big learning for me in my technology job. But in a job that deals with people (such as networking) having fun is hundreds of times more important.

When do you feel most amiable towards another person? Is it when they are dragging their feet to reluctantly do something and looking miserable? No, it is not. It's when they're smiling, laughing, happy. People want to be around other happy people.

The final rule of networking and the debunker of myth number 5 is that networking works much better when you're having fun. If you're not enjoying the networking that you're doing at the moment, find ways to change it until you start enjoying it. If possible, keep changing it until you love networking and until you can't imagine not doing it.

So how do I get started with networking?

Once you know people in the industry, having a coffee one on one is almost always the best way to connect with them. You can discuss their thoughts directly, ask the questions that you are interested in and (perhaps!) discuss potential collaborative projects with them. I find that I manage to find a potential way to collaborate with everyone. These projects don't always come off but they are always a great source of conversation and ideas for the future. In short, by having a coffee with someone you have their undivided attention and you can take advantage of it. I read a lovely article recently by someone in the publishing industry who called this the "secret coffee" way of networking, which I think is quite sweet.

But where do you meet the people to have coffee with? The best way to do this is via on and off-line communities. I belong to several, all of which have been helpful to me in various ways and each of which are good for meeting particular types of people.

Coming from the tech community, I have had a lot of experience with networking groups set up for women. Women are in a minority in the tech industry and over the last ten years or so lots of people have recognised this and built up support groups. So transferring this idea over to the acting world, one group that I joined early on was a group called Women in Film and TV. The challenges for women working in film are slightly different. Unlike in technology there are many more women taking part, but there are fewer women on our screens (research shows that both drama and factual programmes show men to women at a ratio of 2:1) and very few women in the top creative roles such as film directing.

Women in Film and TV hold great networking events for women who work in all roles across both industries and specialist meetup groups for writers, actors and other skillsets.

Obviously not everyone can join Women in Film and TV (sorry guys) but in such a large industry it is always worth looking for small groups that you relate to. There are more Black and Minority Ethnic (BAME) groups springing up as people have started to recognise and address this imbalance in the industry (again both on and off-screen). One day I would like to set up a group for people who do acting and coding, so drop me a line if you're interested in joining that group!

There are lots of organisations that are primarily comprised of actors. Each of the places that are good for training – The Actors Centre, The Actors Guild, etc. – tend to also have networking and social events. The UK Actors Tweetup holds regular events. I'm sure there are many more. It's often a good idea to google "actors meetups" or similar to find new ones that are springing up.

Because I am always looking to start new collaborative projects, I prefer to network within groups where there are a wider range of people looking to meet others. Shooting People is a fantastic site for this. You need to pay to join the community and then there are online job postings and also people posting at an earlier stage when they are looking for someone to work with to write a new series, or help at an earlier stage with a project.

Shooting People works really well because most people on there are starting out too. It can be a much better experience as a starting out actor to work with a starting out director and DOP and so on. You work together as a team to make something happen. Shooting People also organises networking drinks – Shooters in the Pub – around the countries that they operate in. There are many groups all over the UK, not just in London.

I mentioned earlier the great group that I belong to called London Film Collaborative. Even though this is in many ways a subset of Shooting People, because it is smaller people can get to know each other better and form real relationships. You should always be on the lookout for great small groups – or if you can't find one, why not start one yourself?

As you become more popular, more people will hear about you. This is an amazing position to be in because then you need to do less active networking and can to a certain extent wait for the networking to come to you!

As an actor, or anyone with a public profile, it's important to take charge of this. What do people find about you when they search on the web? Do they find your personal website? Or maybe they find your Twitter feed or Facebook page. As you register with sites like Casting Call Pro and get credits on IMDB those pages will start to appear in a search against your name too.

If people hear about you, or meet you at an event, and think of you for a project they may well Google you. What impression will they get from this? If people find a site that clearly states that you are an actor, with good headshots, a showreel (if possible) and (of course!) contact details, then they are more likely to get in touch.

I do understand that this may conflict with the image of yourself that you need people to find when they search on you for your day job. I describe myself on different platforms in various ways depending on who I think is most likely to find me there. On Twitter my description is "Film actor, MD @SoftwireUK, technology & backgammon expert (BBC Click, WSOB, Shoreditch Radio), author Networking Know-How (@urbanepublications)." (i.e. actor first), whereas on LinkedIn my title appears first as "Managing Director, Softwire" and you have to scroll through several other business roles before you will find out that I'm an actor.

It's also worth thinking about how you will keep in touch with the people that you meet. As I'm writing this, this is a particularly sore point for me as I haven't been able to find a platform that allows me to easily keep in touch with all the fabulous people that I meet in the acting world. For business, I use LinkedIn and I find that most business people are on there. LinkedIn sends me updates from my connections, for example when they change jobs, but mostly it allows me to keep everyone I meet in a massive online address book. This is so much more useful than business cards, plus I get access to their entire CV when I want to check whether they are the right contact for me to introduce to someone else.

I find that actors and directors that I meet are rarely on LinkedIn. Lots of actors link up on Facebook, both in direct one to one relationships and as members of groups. Facebook doesn't have the same ease of use as LinkedIn for me and I don't find it as easy to recollect past acquaintances because there is not so much detail on the profiles. Similarly with Twitter. I could create Twitter lists and add directors to one, actors to another, writers to a third etc. but I don't think it would give me what I am looking for.

I have become a member of two connecting platforms designed for the film industry. Slated and Stage 32 are both sites that were started in the US but have expanded to have global reach. Slated is all about film investment, so perhaps it will become more useful to me once I am planning my indie feature film blockbuster, but at the moment I have only a single friend on there – my friend Maria Ingold who invited me.

On Stage 32 I have the opposite problem. Everyone is clearly interested in expanding their networks and are very friendly, perhaps too friendly! I get several requests to connect every month and as a result I have a network where I know **not one** of the people I am connected to in real life. When I have tried to connect to people I know they have not responded, which I think is because they have been similarly overwhelmed by people they don't know and hence are not using the platform. (Or they don't like me after all.)

Many actors manage to get along with their acting work while hating the concept of networking. You don't need to be a good networker in order to make productions and get them out there. Acting is a competitive business though, and you need as much as you can to get ahead. Why not give networking a go – in my style of course, where you have fun and be genuinely yourself – and see if it can become another string to your bow?

Interview – Paul Clayton

Paul Clayton is a TV, theatre and film actor best known as Sophie's dad in Peep Show and Graham in Him and Her. He's the Chairman of The Actors Centre in London and a columnist for The Stage.

"We have so many resources now. As a boy I was cutting up shoeboxes and making toy soldiers tell stories. I wonder what it would have been like if we had iMovie. I remember dragging people at school into the corner of playgrounds to put on plays. That's what I've always tried to do, to do something that I have ownership over.

My father did a bit of Amdram long before I came along (it wasn't something he pursued). I thought he was the person least likely to be an actor. So I don't know where it came from but it was always there. I did a little play when I was 7, in the top year of infant school. It was called Evil Spirits and it involved a soldier, a witch, a maiden and a baby. Envelope breaking for its time. The people in it were forced to be in it and we did it in Mrs Bentham's class on a Friday afternoon. I remember it as a great saga but it was probably 6 minutes long.

It was the thing of holding a room captive and I thought I like this. I remember doing humpty dumpty and it was so good the teacher said we'll do it for the whole school. I was wearing my mother's wedding dress as the queen, in front of 150 people and they were laughing and I thought I want to do this. This is where I want to be. It made things really easy. Other people were having to work out what they wanted to do but I had no question.

I knew that you had to go to drama school. We didn't have the internet. There was one dog-eared pamphlet in the careers room called jobs in drama and I think that had the names of drama schools in it. There was a poster that came with it about auditions for the National Youth Theatre. I got in in 1974. I found myself in London with Tim Spall, Alex Jennings and Caroline Langrishe. I met a lot of like-minded people. That was what convinced me that someone from South Yorkshire could come to London and do this.

It must be very different now with the internet, you can sit in Nottingham and feel in touch with it. There are far too many people applying to drama school and they are taking too many people; more than can ever make a living from it. The good thing was in my day the knowledge was much less available. I applied for RADA and I got in. Then my mother started looking at the costs and I realised my parents weren't as wealthy as I thought they were (they had two shops in Yorkshire). So I had to go somewhere I would get a grant and the only place was Manchester Polytechnic. So I went there.

After this is where it comes down to luck. I was very lucky that in my final year the new assistant director of the Royal Exchange theatre came to drama school to direct me in Hedda Gabler and I got on really well with him. I was given really nice parts; they were older parts – the big heavy older leads. We did a showcase in Manchester at the Royal Exchange as well as London. He came up to me in the car park and he gave me an envelope with a job offer for a 16 week tour of Europe in A Winter's Tale followed by an eight week run at the Royal Exchange. I was paid £68/week and it was brilliant.

In those days you wrote to reps (repertory theatres) and a combination of that and being seen in shows was how I got work. I notice working with young graduates today they are thinking "who's my agent?". Not "Where's the job?". The agent just becomes someone to blame. Our focus was on getting jobs not getting agents. None of us got snapped up by agents.

Four years later in 1982 my friend Pippa's agent came to see her in Leicester. The agent sent a postcard afterwards and at the bottom it said "Does Paul Clayton have an agent?". So I acquired an agent and then I had the longest period out of work that I'd ever had. I'd been working reasonably solidly and then I didn't work for nine months from January to September 1982.

It was just because she changed the things I was going up for. I got close for two leads in the West End but I'd never had experience of those sorts of interviews. I'm sure I talked my way out of one by telling them my true age – they thought I was older. It's important to enter the meeting on an equal footing rather than just being interrogated. You have to give yourself the status in the room – it's you that gets you work not your acting. It can be things you can't think of that make people make the decision. I remember when it got to the stage when I was sitting behind the desk as a director, I thought the reason I am not going to go for you is one that hasn't even entered your head. Those are the skills that are so key to your success. No-one can teach you to act, but they can teach you to be an actor. Those skills are really key to how you do.

I always played older. The problem at the start of my career was that I wasn't old enough. Although I did some really nice stuff in my twenties, I spent most of my thirties directing and then for no reason when I hit forty it took off and when I hit fifty it all fell into place. So many young actors feel that if they don't work by Christmas it will all be over. You are running a marathon not the hundred metres. I'd have been terrible if I'd been successful in my 20s – I drank a lot and I would have dealt with it really badly. Now I have some success (touching wood); I'm a financial success, I'm in the lucky position that people have seen my stuff and liked it and in my personal life I'm happy. I appreciate it every day."

MONEY

The profession of acting is in a decline, or a boom, depending on whether you are looking at it from the point of view of wanting to make a living from it, or from the opposite view of needing a plentiful supply of cheap actors. Last year, based on data released by the actors' union Equity, the Telegraph revealed that over half of all actors are living below the poverty line, with the Independent posting an even starker figure: only 1 in 20 professional actors earns over £20,000 – a basic starting salary in many other industries. Malcolm Sinclair, the president of Equity, was quoted as saying "Compared to when I started there are so many more drama schools, and university courses. There are far more young actors coming out and it feels like there is less work around. There are too many actors and too few jobs."

The cause of this lack of jobs, paid jobs that is, seems, ironically, to be a consequence of the age of plenty in which we currently live. Fifty or even just twenty years ago, it was tough to make it as an actor, but it felt possible. Now it feels that the only thing achievable is a life of hard knocks and penury. This era of plenty started, again ironically, with the golden age of cinema. Before cinema if you wanted to be entertained by actors, they needed to be in the same room as you and if more than fifty, or a few hundred, of you wanted to see the show they needed to do it again and again and again. One of the most missed aspects of actor training (and one that sadly will not be coming back, no matter how much we mourn it) is the repertory theatre. In rep a troupe of actors plays a new show each week, working together (often) for years and honing their craft to a diamond-like sheen of brilliance. The coming of the film meant that you could make a reproducible copy of a single show (I'm simplifying). This copy could then be distributed out to be played all across the world, with no actors needed beyond the initial shoot!

The golden age of cinema did of course create new opportunities for actors too. Because a single film could bring in such a large revenue, there was the possibility of high fees for those actors lucky enough to become a star and good wages paid for co-stars, smaller parts and for work in the new television industry. Creating a film or a television show was a super expensive endeavour, requiring loads of complex kits and a large crew to operate it. Then more recently along came smaller cameras, which were suddenly quite good, and then mobile telephones, that allowed you to film anything anywhere entirely on your own. In 2016, anyone can become a filmmaker and distribute their film to the largest audience in the world via YouTube.

But, wait. Shouldn't ease of filmmaking mean more jobs for actors, not fewer? Well that depends on what you mean by job. If you want to act for free in a web series or a student film then yes it does. If you wish to be able to eat and pay for somewhere to live solely on income that you earn by acting then no, no it does not. Not by a long way. In fact... ease of shooting; makes cheaper shoots possible; increases downwards pressure on budgets; means fewer paid jobs for actors. Oh and cheap reality TV formats didn't help much either.

So is everything gloomy for anyone's chances as an actor? Maybe if you want to be rich and famous, but we all know that isn't the end game anyway. If you want to be an actor for the life and the experiences, then I'm not so sure that the future is gloomy at all. In fact in many ways, it's quite the opposite.

Lots of highly visible and influential creative people are coming out and saying on the record that earning a living from your creativity is not the mark of whether your creativity is worthwhile or not. The creative world is not like the business world where we all have regular jobs. There are no "regular jobs" in acting (unless you're lucky enough to become a series regular on a long-running soap) in the same way that there are no regular jobs if you are a painter, or an author or a playwright.

A few years ago I wrote an article on whether musicians should work for free for the fabulous alternative music magazine Alt-Mu. While thinking through the issues I realised something that has become fundamental to the way that I think about acting and money. I believe that commerce and creativity are inherently at odds with each other.

What is it that makes something creative? I'd like to suggest that the main criteria, the one that stands out above all others, is that the act is free of coercion. Art is made when people engage with their materials, whatever those may be, in an act of spontaneous creation. We have all had that feeling of doing something that we love, and many of us have found that we can lose that feeling if we start being "expected" to deliver what we were previously doing for fun. Art is what you do when no-one is telling you what to do.

Let's look at making money from our art, which so many people dream of. I'll stick with painting as an example. If you want to make a living as a painter, you will not be able to achieve this by sitting in a dark room on your own, painting. You will need to bring your paintings out to where people can buy them. Perhaps you will need to sell them yourself on a market stall, or perhaps you will have a sales agent – but then you will need to acquire and deal with the sales agent.

Let's assume that you don't change what or how you paint in order to sell more (although in that case you need to get lucky that people like what you do). Even so you will now have acts that create art i.e. doing the actual painting, and acts that turn it into money – running the stall or having meetings with people who do this work on your behalf. As soon as you start trying to earn a living from your craft, it becomes commerce rather than art.

Elizabeth Gilbert, the bestselling author of Eat, Pray, Love recently released a book, Big Magic, talking about her experiences of the creative process. She rather charmingly likens it to catching ideas that are floating around invisibly. She explains how it was not until she had written her fourth published book that she was able to give up work and live from her writing, and that book was the multi-million bestseller Eat, Pray, Love.

Gilbert believes that adding pressure to yourself to achieve financial goals via your creativity will block you from achieving your full potential. She has a lovely quote that sums this up. "To yell at your creativity, saying, 'You must earn money for me!' is sort of like yelling at a cat: it has no idea what you're talking about, and all you're doing is scaring it away, because you're making really loud noises and your face looks weird when you do that."

Something else that comes in to play when trying to earn a living from acting, is that not all acting roles are created equal. It seems to be generally true that the more creative and fulfilling a role is, the less likely you are to be paid for it. The most well paid roles in acting are usually in commercials – looking at a beach and laughing or holding a cup of coffee and looking seductively at your neighbour. There are not many actors who went into the job for this! Similarly actors often end up taking "corporate role play" jobs, helping businesses to explain concepts to their employees. A job that needs acting skills, certainly and one that can be interesting in its own way. But it's not Shakespeare.

I think that a better way to think about how you earn a living is to put everything on a sliding scale. Weigh up each activity that you do and work out how much you enjoy it. If you enjoy it more, you can earn less from it, whereas if you don't enjoy it very much you should only do it if it pays well.

I am in an extremely lucky position where I actually like my day job. So when looking at acting opportunities I weight up three things.

1. How much does it pay? (Or cost me, in many cases!)
2. How much will I learn from it?
3. How useful will it be as a CV credit?

And obviously I also think about how much fun it will be. If something doesn't work for me under points 2 & 3 then it would need to pay more than my day job in order for me to consider it. So I rarely apply for commercials or corporate work because it's not really what I want to do and won't help me in getting drama work in the future.

When you're calculating how much you get paid for a piece of acting work, it's worth considering any hidden costs. One key one is the time taken to audition. If I get paid £200 for a day shoot for a commercial, and I get cast roughly every 5 auditions and each audition takes two hours of my time, that the effective rate that I am being paid is less than £100/day.

Often employers add in other hidden costs too, such as expecting you to attend a rehearsal or planning meeting for free. Then of course there is any time spent learning lines or preparing for the shoot. I'm not trying to knock employers here – they are operating under tight budgets too – but just pointing out that if something takes up a lot of your time, it might not be the great income generation activity that you thought it was.

On the subject of employers, having now produced a few shows I have quite a good insight into how much money is made from fringe theatre. The answer is "not very much". It's really easy to feel underpaid and undervalued as an actor, especially if lots of people are asking you to work for expenses only. It's only when you look at it from the other side of trying to put a show on that you realise how expensive a business it is.

First up you need to pay for the venue. Some shows can be put on in venues that are happy to let you play for free. I really recommend developing this kind of show if you are starting out in production. The downside of a free venue is that there won't be much available in terms of technical theatre support – lights, sound and so on. If you need a professional theatre set up with different lighting states (which can add a lot of depth to a production) then you will need to hire a purpose built theatre. Hiring a venue starts at a minimum of £500/week, and that is for a "half slot" where two plays run one after the other on the same evening.

If you want to work with a professional director, the Equity rate for directing a play is £1000/week. If this is not explicitly put aside for the director then they are either working for less (or free), or are perhaps doing some other roles too (e.g. producer) so they are earning a living that way.

Then there are other costs: props, technicians, travel and other assorted expenses that crop up.

Looking at the revenue side of a show, it is hard to make things add up. How much can you sell a ticket for? Fringe tickets for short shows rarely sell for more than £10-15. So assuming a ticket price of £10, you need to sell 50 tickets/week just to pay for the venue. You can make more money if you have a longer run. Two months of a full house at £10/ticket and you can very possibly afford to pay everyone and make a profit.

How easy is it to sell 1000 tickets for a fringe show? That requires marketing staff and marketing expenses for fliers, posters, adverts etc. i.e. more cost…. Suffice to say if a fringe theatre producer ever offers you "profit share", don't bank on getting any payment!

Given how hard it is to make a living from acting, almost all actors have to take other jobs in order to pay the rent. Common jobs that actors take include bar staff, waiter, office manager, barista, corporate trainer or actors often work in theatres, on films and in general odd jobs. These tend to be casual jobs i.e. you can pick them up and put them down quite easily. This is great for acting because you never know when you'll be needed for an audition or for a production.

On the other hand these jobs are not so great since they tend to be poorly paid, and often are not very satisfying. Rather than being something that is different from acting, and also a meaningful part of your life, they feel like they are simply a way to pass the time while you wait for your acting career to "take off".

I believe you can and should have more than this. No-one is a one trick pony, a one skill person. I wholeheartedly encourage everyone to follow their love of acting, and I also believe that everyone also has many, many other talents and skills that they can enjoy using. And I believe that some of those skills will make money.

I am in an unusual and extremely lucky position where I have (kind of accidentally) built a career outside of acting. This means that I have a great day job that I enjoy doing when I am not acting. It is also a career rather than just a job – I continue to learn skills and increase my potential in this area. I think that having something where you can build and grow and develop is one of the things that makes a job satisfying. If you are just doing the same thing over and over again to earn a quick buck it will never be as rewarding.

You might be in the same position as me where you have a job that you love. If so, amazing! Now you just need to find a way to make it work with acting. There are lots of books with recommendations on how to make a part-time job from a full-time job, so I won't go into more detail here. The 4 Hour Work Week by Tim Ferris is a great starting point.

Or you might have a job that you hate. In that case I recommend focussing some of your energy on changing it into a job that you love and can develop in. This might mean getting a new job. You also have the opportunity to start thinking about whether you can build your own business or a freelance career, which will give you freedom to pursue acting while also having a rewarding stable source of income. Marianne Caldwell's brilliant book "How to be a Free Range Human" has some good ideas in this area.

If you are in the (perhaps) enviable position of not yet having a job because you are studying, I strongly recommend looking for something that is flexible, well-paid and with learning potential (and hence increased salary potential). I didn't do it deliberately, but the fact that I have ended up with a job that meets these three criteria is making my acting experiment much less stressful.

In life it's always good to be as self-reliant as possible in terms of being able to generate your own opportunities. This is doubly true in acting. Lots of the worst bits of the acting industry (and even more so in modelling – I've heard proper horror stories) happen because actors are prepared to let themselves be dependent on powerful others.

Having another source of income is a fantastic way to be more self-reliant. Not only are you not desperate for acting gigs in order to pay the rent (and being desperate puts pressure on you in an audition and makes it hard for you to do your best), but you can also afford to work for free occasionally, and invest in showreel and other opportunities.

You're also likely to be less miserable and feel more alive. A happy actor is a good actor.

Interview – Nick Cohen

Nicholas Cohen is an actor and a film director, producer and writer. He has directed Eastenders and Doctors for TV as well as several feature films.

"I used to put on plays for my parents, for example 'Eggs for the Easter Bunny'. I remember drawing all of the programmes by hand – these were almost as exciting as the play. I'd just learnt how to make frozen lollies in the freezer for the interval. I remember more about the programmes and putting lollies through the little dumbwaiter hatch than what was in the play.

At primary school I remember being Herod. The teacher said "You must all speak up. Apart from Nicholas who could be a bit quieter." I was going to be Charlie in Charlie and the Chocolate Factory but I had an accident and cut my eye open and needed stitches so I lost the part. I guess it's one of the funny things about show business, how precarious everything is. I've been an understudy at the RSC (Royal Shakespeare Company) and ended up playing so many parts, and I've had to cast people at the last minute. It's all so precarious. Opportunities come up and disappear. It can drive you bonkers; you have to have a philosophical mindset or maybe an opportunistic mindset – you might get a call at any time. It's really quite zen; you need to let go of the idea that the harder you try the further you'll get.

I acted all through school and university. At Cambridge University you already feel like you're doing it professionally. You go to the Edinburgh Fringe and the European Theatre Group and the Marlowe society put on four shows a year at the Cambridge Arts Theatre. Plus there's the ADC Theatre. You feel like you're hovering on the edge of the profession.

I was always torn between acting and directing, even at school and uni and in the end I went into directing. It's good to have directing and writing as well as acting. In fact it would be even better to have something completely different that's calm and reliable and reminds you that acting's not life and death and that there are more things in the world. The world of theatre and film can make you really unbalanced as a person. You have a distorted, adrenalised view of life.

One of my favourite times was when I was on tour with the RSC. It was the first time the RSC ever went to India. I was the assistant director and understudy. I went with director Tim Supple to the Taj Mahal. It was amazing. I got back and there was a show that night and they said 'Gary's sick, you're on as Balthazar in A Comedy of Errors'. There was a sword fight and I had an hour to learn the moves. I had been covering all the parts and Gary was never sick so I had to learn the fight and the lines at the last minute. There was a huge audience in Delhi of over four thousand people and the Governor of Delhi was in. It was such an adrenaline rush. I got laughs that Gary had never got and that feeling was incredible.

Half the time in the past I only made a quite basic living. In lean years I lived on less money than many people would think is possible. I rarely bought CDs, books or clothes. I don't eat meat; I don't drink alcohol; I don't have a car. I'm stringent about phone and internet providers. I have a lifestyle that accommodates lean years. It becomes more and more difficult the older you get, effectively living like a student. It's OK, but for example, I would like to have a family. When I'm dating someone there is a misunderstanding that because I've directed Eastenders, and at the National – they don't realise that doesn't always pay particularly well and then there are gaps on top of that. It's getting harder and harder because in the independent film world the collapse of DVD means it's harder to make a living there.

I worked with someone called Jonathan Kay who's a maverick practitioner. He did a lot of street theatre and street festivals and theatre by donation. It was interesting to see how you can earn money that way. You don't have to be in the conventional space – you can be more agile and fluid. Sometimes I would do an improvised show with Jonathan and make a lot of money, more than you'd expect. If you market an event as a scratch show and don't charge too much money, it means that you can't make much money from it. Whereas if something is by donation and it's an 'event' then lots of people turn up and you can make a lot of money.

In order to exist in this precarious insecure world, rather than try it out and get disheartened by how arbitrary it is, you do need a certain amount of base level confidence and robustness. My best friend is the actor James Callis, who plays the gay best mate in Bridge Jones. He recently shot Bridget Jones 3, he's playing a baddie in The Three Musketeers etc etc – he's a very successful actor. He has a beautiful house in LA, has both a great UK agent and a great American agent, but he still faces rejection. For him it's like water off a duck's back. He doesn't even notice (most of the time). That robustness is completely at odds with the sensitivity and imagination that you need as an actor. That's why I'm more comfortable career wise being a director – I couldn't cope with the constant rejection. You do develop more detachedness and robustness as you get older, which is a good argument for entering acting later in life."

TIME

Time is a difficult existential concept. Many people believe that time doesn't exist, and that was before the whole idea was blown apart when it became a kind of extension of space as part of the space-time continuum. What is time when you look closely at it? Like many things the closer you look, the more it seems to disappear.

This isn't a theoretical treatise. Whatever time is, it's is relevant to acting in all kinds of ways.

Age

One of the best things about The Artist's Way, the fabulous book for unblocking creative people written by Julia Cameron and the book that started me on this journey, is that it lists out all the ways that we stop ourselves from doing things and it debunks them one by one. It's fabulous to read through the list and realise that you're doing it yourself.

It's great to have someone tell you in a no-nonsense but kindly tone that these are just excuses in your head and that you can ignore them and get on with doing what you want to do. Like a kind of virtual parent or other kindly relative.

The biggest excuse that we use to tell ourselves that we can't do something is our age. I think that there are many good reasons for this. We look around at people who are portrayed on TV and think about whether that could be us. (Where are all the women over 40?) We read the celebrity interviews with actors who knew from a young age that acting was all that they wanted to pursue and after years training in youth theatres and drama schools, and then after tens of years of working their way up slowly, they gradually got a break.

How tempting to try to apply that to yourself, as you are right now, and come to a seemingly inexorable conclusion that it is "too late".

What starts to debunk this for me is that people of all ages seem to believe that it is "too late" for them. I have started out at acting aged 35. I am undecided about whether I am "too late" or "just in time". There are many, many positive things about starting acting at the age that I am now, but I'll never be the beautiful 20-something lead in a film. Then again, is that what I really want?

Once you start to break these things down you find that there are a lot of assumptions (not just about age) that get in the way of doing what your soul tells you is right.

I am particularly influenced in my conviction that 35 was not too late at all, by my experience as a 23-year-old that I mentioned earlier in the book. Having loved acting as a child but having been too shy, I suddenly realised aged twenty-three that all I had needed to do was to work harder, try harder and keep going. "But," I reflected, "woe is me. If only I had known that when I was twelve I could have done something about now. Now it is far far too late." Far too late! Aged twenty-three! Imagine it! I'm sure that 47-year-old Zoe would have the same reaction if she were looking back to 35-year-old Zoe thinking it's too late.

It is true that we live in a culture that worships youth, especially for women. There's a difference between trying to change the film industry for the better in this regard (which many great female actors are working very hard to do) and using the way the world is as a block to stop you from following your dreams.

As well as being seen as a vehicle for fame (which is an insubstantial reason for wanting to act), acting (and especially film acting) is often seen in a similar vein to modelling, as a rubber stamp of approval on how you look. This is also an insubstantial reason for wanting to act. By insubstantial I mean that this is a reason that isn't going to make you happy in the long run.

I truly believe that people who are following their dreams and living their live to the full are happier than those who are too timid or cautious to give things a go. I have never met someone who was hungry for fame or outside approval who was happy. These are wants that only ever grow. The more you feed them (i.e. by getting cast or getting approval in another way) the more they want. They simply get bigger and bigger.

The saddest thing of all is that all of the inside feelings that go along with young women's quests for fame are usually hidden. All we see is the success and the beautiful photos and we think that they must be happy. People around the world were touched recently when Essena O'Neill, a sixteen-year-old with 500,000 Instagram followers, deleted her account and posted about how unhappy posing for perfect photos had made her. It seems obvious now that she has come out and said it, but until then she was considered as something to aspire to for young women – healthy and smiling. But the photos didn't tell the truth.

So if you're thinking that maybe you are too old to start on an acting career, have another think. Perhaps it is an advantage that you are not young and naïve. You are less likely to get caught up in the shallow side of acting and more likely to find challenging and interesting parts. As German TV actress Michaela Merten, once said to me. "Directors cast leading females that they are a little bit in love with. This means that women fear losing their looks and focus on the wrong things in acting. Luckily you are at no risk of that happening with you." Ha ha ha ha ha.

So I am at peace with the fact that by the time I have done enough training, I'll be in my 40s. Acting is not modelling. In many ways we just transfer the hangups that we focus on in everyday life across to acting, where they are even less relevant.

As part of the process of applying for acting roles, you constantly need to choose photos and videos to represent yourself. Assuming you can get past looking at yourself over and over again (very few people enjoy looking at pictures of themselves and yes, that includes most actors) you're still likely not to make a very good choice when it comes to picking a photo.

We've all been brought up to try to choose photos where we look "nice". We try to get a camera shot of our attractive side, or that catches us in just the one position where we look stunning. And that is not the best photo for acting. The casting director wants to see a photo that genuinely represents you and what you look like. It is no good if you send off a photo taken five years ago of you wearing a ton of makeup and then rock up looking completely different.

More importantly, casting directors are not looking for people who look nice. Looking nice, especially nowadays, implies a kind of bland acceptable level of attractiveness. Our nice photos are the ones where our nose doesn't look too big, where our skin is clear and blemish free, where our hair stayed put in the shape we wanted. This is what nice is, and it's no use at all for a film.

Casting directors are looking for character. They are looking for people with character and therefore they are looking for photos that depict people with character. Not people who look nice. This is why actors are advised whenever possible to let someone else choose their photos. I can't wait until I get a manager and can ask them to pick for me!

A couple of times recently when I have told people that I am starting to pursue acting, they have paid me an amazing compliment – that I have an interesting face. It's taken me a while to recognise this as compliment. In everyday life "interesting" is used as a euphemism. To be told I have an interesting face means I am not winning any beauty contests any time soon. For acting it is just the opposite. The worst thing you can have is a bland face. And don't forget that character develops with age.

The thing that best convinces me that it is not "too late" for anyone and that no-one is "too old" is that plenty of people cut themselves off by believing exactly the opposite. The world is full of people who believe that they are too young to pursue their dreams, be happy, get what they want. And given how crazy that sounds to me, it makes me realise that thinking you are too old is just as wrong.

Experience

I can still remember when I first started out as an actor. I had a good few months of auditioning for several plays and being cast in nothing. I was used to pushing myself in my day job by making plans and taking next steps. But here I was suddenly unable to enact my plans because I couldn't get myself cast in anything. I felt like time was slipping away from me. I felt that if something didn't happen soon then I'd have to give up on acting altogether.

Looking back from my vantage point now I can see that this was an inevitable part of my learning. I also see that things simply don't happen in a linear fashion when you are developing acting skills. I could even have pushed myself less and spent a longer period of time doing more auditions and with fewer results. Even then, by sticking with it in the long term shoots will start to grow and things will start to happen.

At the start of your career when you have no credits, no showreel and perhaps only a few photos it feels like a mammoth task to get to where you want to be. It feels like a big job just to get to a point that you can start from!

It will happen. It just takes time. And you need to stick with it and help it happen in the same way as everything else, by taking one small step after another until you get there.

Talking of steps reminds me a really beautiful analogy that I just read in a book called "The Inner Game of Tennis" by Timothy Gallwey. It's not a book about acting, but it has some great insights into how humans learn and develop skills. Reading it, I could see the parallels with my own journey becoming an actor.

Gallwey found that people in general were not doing very well at learning tennis. They would get an instruction from a coach, say "lift your back arm higher" and then they would try to put this into practice. They would attempt to try to play better tennis by a series of verbal instructions that they then repeated to themselves, internally beating themselves up when they couldn't get it right. "Why are you still raising your arm too high, you idiot?"

Beating yourself up doesn't increase your tennis learning. In fact Gallwey found that on the contrary "telling yourself what to do" gets in the way of your body's natural ability to learn new skills. He also suggests that beating yourself up for not being at a more advanced stage of learning is not a great response in general and he likens it to a child learning to walk. When a child is learning to walk they stumble and fall and pick themselves up and fall again. No-one ever says "how come you can't walk already, you idiot?". Instead they smile and laugh and encourage the child, while marvelling at children's inbuilt capacity to learn.

Like learning to walk, Gallwey thinks that we can learn to play tennis by letting go and seeing what happens rather than by trying to instruct ourselves. And I think a similar approach can be useful for acting. So don't beat yourself up just because you're starting out!

In fact there can be many positive things associated with being a beginner. I still spend time deliberately reminding myself of these, which gives me the strength to carry on when I find the going tough, or I'm trying to stretch myself by doing things above my current skill level.

When you are a beginner you have nothing to lose. It doesn't feel like that. Everything is scary and new and it feels like you can completely make a fool of yourself and lose the right to ever do acting. But actually all you have to lose is one bad experience, then you can pick yourself up and start again.

It gets much harder the more successful you are. You have more to lose – agents, contacts, reputation. And (I hear) the fear of failure doesn't go away. So enjoy the fact that when you fall it won't be too far.

There is a lovely concept in mindfulness meditation called beginners' mindset. It refers to the idea that we can really benefit from looking at things anew, as if we have never encountered them before. We build up so much baggage around something once we have got accustomed to it. We can miss subtleties or new angles that could be gained from different vantage points. So it is great to be able to return to the beginners' mindset.

So, big, big advantage to being an actual beginner – you get beginners' mindset for free! You don't even have to try. Everything will be fresh and new. You will be unencumbered by outmoded ideas about acting, or ways that you have been trained that no longer work for you. Enjoy it!

Also there is a certain amount of fun and energy that comes from being at the start of a journey. You have no idea what could happen! It is all tremendously exciting.

Psychologists have documented four stages of learning. First is unconscious incompetence, then conscious incompetence, then conscious competence and finally unconscious competence. You start in unconscious incompetence. This can be bliss.

I did my first one-woman show with hardly any experience (a couple of short films and two short acting courses). I was scared but I really had no concept of the undertaking that I was setting out on. A one-woman show was just an accessible form of acting that was easy for me to make happen.

I've since learned that very experienced and well trained actors often quake at the thought of performing on their own in this way. When you are performing on your own you need to personally sustain all of the energy and commitment required to make a show work. It all has to come from you. In a larger production you can hide to a certain extent behind the director, or lose yourself in interacting with other actors. There is nowhere to hide in a one person show. As a complete beginner, I was blithely unaware of all of this and consequently it couldn't phase me.

It's worth remembering that another thing that you get "for free" when you are starting out is a new and fresh perspective. As you train and become more and more competent you also, by definition become more and more like everyone else. You become more similar to the actors who have had similar training and experiences to you. The more you know, the more people you are acting in a similar way to.

There's a reason that people love bright young things in the arts. It's not to do with their age, but to do with the fact that it is from these people that the most new, different, dynamic and exciting works come. Their success is a result of their lack of experience, not despite it.

The more you can enjoy being a beginner and the more you can focus on bringing whatever you have to your art rather than bemoaning what you lack, the more easily you will transition, slowly and almost imperceptibly, into a skilled and authentic artist. If you are always looking ahead or at other people you will lose your own uniqueness and your work will become derivative.

To everything there is a season. Everything that you want to be able to do now will come in time. You can see the evidence for this if you look closely while you are on your journey. Watch out for the small, subtle and yet significant changes that accompany you on your way.

Do you feel differently about attending a class now? Do you have a warmer reaction to other actors – seeing them as fellow travellers rather than competitors? These are small changes. But this is how growth and development works. Our media love "overnight success" stories, but these are always exaggerated and often very, very far from the truth. Behind every overnight success story there is a hidden path of tens of years of work.

Enjoy seeing your craft develop. It is easy to want it all at once, but you will be better able to find the peace and commitment to stick with what will be a challenging path if you learn that it is a long road.

When I started acting, I had a very clear picture of where I wanted to be. I had done a visualisation exercise of a perfect day as part of The Artist's Way. I was living in a high rise flat with a balcony, somewhere very sunny (I would say this was clearly LA, but who knows?). I had breakfast with my husband outside (no perfect life is complete for me unless I get to have breakfast with my husband!) and then spent the rest of the day on set or in other film work.

I knew what I wanted but I didn't know how to get there, so at every step I would take my big picture success idea and compare where I was to that. I felt like I was constantly saying "Am I there yet? Am I there yet?" like a frantic child in the back of a car.

I tried to break what I was doing down into steps or pieces that I could achieve one at a time. It was easy to see which things were dependent on other things. For example I was not going to be able to get an agent until I got some credits and a showreel. There were certain roles it was not worth applying for until I had a showreel. And so on.

So at the start I had some basic building blocks that I knew that I needed and I focussed on getting those. That gave me the wrong idea though. I started to feel that I could break things down into steps. 1. Get good photos. 2. Get credits. 3. Get showreel. 4. Make connections. 5. Get an agent. 6. Get more credits.

Despite starting to tick these off, I felt that I wasn't getting any closer to where I wanted to be. I was not 5% of the way to the LA dream (or even 1% or 0.1%). The things I was doing, while clearly useful, did not map across. I tried thinking about what I wanted as a big picture, which was to be "good" at acting. Now not only did I have to compare "Am I good at acting yet?" (No) I also started to ask "Is what I'm doing making me better at acting?". And I found that I had absolutely no idea.

My acting coach (Jeremy Stockwell) resolutely told me that acting did not work in a linear fashion. I was used to planning a career and training for each step, progressing in a nice straightforward manner to the next level. Acting does not work like that.

There are all kinds of motivational quotes up in the Actors Centre in Covent Garden, from established film and theatre actors. Lots of them centre around that the fact that no-one really knows what acting is, how to do it, or how to learn. Another common theme is that everyone is continually learning and developing their craft.

As I've worked more in acting, I've got a much clearer idea about how development works.

Let's imagine that the following is a picture of where I want to get to.

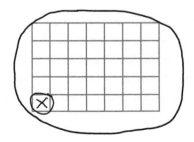

AN ACTOR'S LIFE FOR ME

I'm the small circle around the checked box. I want to get to the big circle. My previous way of learning was to compare where I was to where I wanted to be and see what the difference was. But that wasn't any help. All I learnt was that I was a long way away! That wasn't very motivational.

Instead the key is to realise that you learn in acting by going into more boxes. So everything you do, whether it is a class, a piece of work, a rehearsal or even a life experience (as an actor you are training all the time!) is checking off another box. Sometimes you'll find that you went into the same box, or sometimes it will be slightly different.

The diagram can be a bit misleading, as not all boxes are the same size and not all are equally important. But they're identical in that we can't know how large or important they were until we use them later on. Also, in the diagram there are 35 boxes. In reality, we don't know how many boxes there are and it's unlikely that we will ever check them all off.

I reckon I'm now about here.

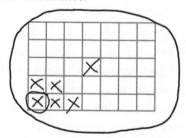

Unlike with my previous way of measuring, where I would just say "Am I there yet?" and get the dispiriting answer "no", I am pretty pleased with the above diagram. I went into some boxes! And I'm learning and improving.

I feel that this plan is completely foolproof going forwards. I intend to follow it forever. As we know from the quotes in the Actors Centre, there is always room for more development and growth. Very often in life, the point at which you stop learning and get stuck is triggered by you deciding you know what you're doing. I instinctively trust people who say that they don't know it all, over those who claim to have it all sewn up. (Where "it" can be acting, or indeed anything in life.)

According to the plan there are only two options: going into boxes, or not going into boxes. There are only two possible reasons to stop going in boxes. The first is if I get scared of going into boxes and give up. (I consider "not having time" or "finding better things to do" to simply be a variation on this theme i.e. an excuse because I am scared.) In this case I have lost.

The second reason for not going into boxes is if I die. But if I die while I was continuing to go into boxes then I have won! I have by definition achieved the most that I can down the acting path. I can't control when I die, I can only control what I do beforehand.

Thinking about this plan has really crystallised for me what I am most scared of. I am most scared that some experience of general lack of progress will dispirit me so much that I give up acting. But in many ways that means that all I am really scared of is not acting. By this logic there is very little for me to fear from acting itself. However lowly the work that I am doing or however badly I feel I am performing, as long as I am acting I am going down the right path.

This may not sound like a very certain or concrete plan. I agree. I have accepted that certainty is not possible and I believe that this is the next best thing. I've come up with this analogy based on what I have found out on my own acting journey. Maybe it is different for you. Maybe there are other ways that you will find to record your successes and progress. If so, brilliant. Part of starting to master any new craft or skill is the process of going from learning from what other people say to being able to define yourself what is right for you in your application of your learning.

If you don't have a plan, and you are finding it hard to track progress (and worrying that you can't), then I do encourage you to think of everything you do as a new block on your acting tower – even if you are repeating something that you've done before you will have a new perspective on it this time. Try to find and celebrate your wins. Look for the things that you find you can do now that you can remember as being impossible at an earlier time.

Whenever I feel down or scared, I often feel that I have made little progress and that any "significant" roles are still beyond me. I find it very comforting to think through the things that seemed impossible to me eighteen months ago, but that, nevertheless, I have achieved.

1. Getting an audition with an agent after they saw me perform in a showcase. When I started out, I was desperate to get an agent. I was so sure that the only way that I would be able to progress my career was with someone else backing me. (This turned out to not be true, of course.) I also needed the validation. I wanted to know that someone else thought I was "good enough" to be worth investing in. This meant that getting involved with agents was an emotional minefield for me. I sent off emails and letters, but rapidly started to feel like I was shouting into a void. I remember really concretely having the feeling that no agent would ever want to see me, which would mean that I'd never get any credits and hence die alone and unloved.

And yet, after being given a great comedy piece for the London Actors Workshop showcase, I got invited to audition by one of the agents on the guest list. (I didn't get accepted, but just getting in to see an agent was a win.)

2. Getting cast from my showreel. Getting a good showreel made was also high up on my list for things that I knew I needed from the get-go. This was a terrible chicken and egg situation. I needed a showreel in order to get auditions for short films, but I needed to be cast in short films in order to get the material to make a showreel.

There is also a perennial problem with your showreel – by the time that you have managed to receive and edit the footage into your showreel, it is already out of date. I met another actor in a play and she said that she had never had a showreel, since by the time she got the footage ready she felt that she had moved on so much that she was embarrassed to use it!

I got really lucky with my first three film credits, which are still the basis of my showreel today (it's now over 12 months old! I'm waiting on some footage from shorts I did last year.). One was the chance encounter with The Look of Love, one was a short film that I did as part of a course with the Actors Centre and one was a 48-hour film competition.

Like with most things that you build up too much, I was super excited when I first got my showreel. It had taken me longer than I anticipated not just to build the credits, but also to actually get hold of the footage and to get it edited. I then waited for the film offers to start rolling in. And I kept waiting.

Soon it felt like it didn't make that much difference having a showreel after all. I started to wonder how good it was and whether anyone even looked at it. I started thinking about how I could get better material and make a better showreel.

And then in July 2015 I was cast in an indie feature film just from my showreel!! I have since been reassured by showing it to my director friends that it is at least "OK", and so despite the fact that I'm still waiting on more footage to make it better, I feel pretty happy about it.

3. Getting cast from a video audition. I've always found self-taped video auditions to be a bit odd. From back when I used to work as a presenter, I've never been much good at self-shooting videos. I always seem to have an "Is it on?" expression.

I do love the fact that self-tape auditions are much lower pressure than auditions in real life. You can do as many takes as you like, and you can choose what the director gets to see. If only I had had an edit facility for some of my live auditions.

Coupled with that, though, is the pressure to get it right, the difficulty of getting the technical side right (by which I mean pressing the start button and making sure the camera is in the right place) and the lack of an outside eye to help with what you are doing. Sometimes self-tapes include dialogue and as I rarely have someone to work with me, I usually make a bit of a mess of those ones.

Luckily (in some ways) I am quite brave, so I always favour sending off something, even if I'm not happy with it. The fact that you rarely get feedback from auditions means that I have no idea how the countless self-tapes I have sent off and not been cast from were received.

It can be hard to keep auditioning into a void and recording yourself and sending off a video is the best example of this. At least in a live (or on a Skype) audition, you can watch for body language, intonation and choice of words to try to figure out how you did. I was sure that video auditions were just something else that I wasn't very good at until I eventually got cast from one!

Like many of the acting things that work best, it was recorded when I took the pressure off myself. I was waiting for a rehearsal and figured that sitting on a bench outside the school where we practised was as good a place as any to make a tape. I don't know exactly what I did that was different, but I was really happy with what I managed to convey in a few takes and then delighted when I got an email saying that I'd been cast. I hadn't been cast as the young mother that I applied for, but instead as a "crone" – but hey, a part's a part!

4. Getting cast from a live audition. My favourite ever moment at a live audition was waiting to go in at the Calder Bookshop Theatre opposite the Young Vic in Southwark. There is a fantastic quote above the entrance to the theatre – "Anyone can act, even actors;

and you can do theatre anywhere, even in theatres. Augusto Boal". I cannot think of a better quote to simultaneously inspire and remind you to get over yourself. (I didn't get cast.)

I am not good at live auditions. This is a fact. I get nervous and I worry too much about what the director wants rather than what I think I should do and very often I completely forget what I am doing. A great example was a simple audition for a one-night new writing showcase. I was asked about my character motivation and what they were trying to achieve and then asked to run the scene again. I totally aced the "answering the questions" bit – "My character is suspicious of the lady she is interviewing and is trying to catch her out and see her reaction." But then I *totally forgot to actually do this* when running the scene. I realised at the end. Doh! (I didn't get cast.)

You can read more about my auditioning ineptitude in the auditions section.

And yet… Next week I start rehearsals for a play that I got through a live audition. Amazing! The only way that I can explain what was different about this audition was a) luck (everyone gets a break sometimes, right?) and b) I managed to totally not care or prep at all for the audition. I had to give a monologue. I asked whether I could do Shakespeare, which I was learning for a RADA Shakespeare exam (an aside: anyone can apply to be tested by RADA on their Shakespeare in return for a bronze, silver or gold medal. I have bronze! And I will apply for silver next time I have some downtime in performances.). It was a totally irrelevant monologue: Imogen from Cymbeline basically talking about how in love she was – this was an audition for a sadistic mental hospital doctor.

I had to wait for 30 minutes as I was early. I did no relaxation prep, monologue prep or other sorts of prep. I focussed on forgetting I was waiting for an audition and read a novel and drank a cup of tea.

I was asked after I did my impression of an eighteen-year-old in love, whether I had a more suitable monologue. I said no and so they asked me to do it again, but more angrily, like I hated everyone. I had never even considered this as a possible interpretation! As a result I had quite a good time in the audition and felt like I was just mucking about.

Articles explaining audition technique are everywhere. Lots of courses that I have taken emphasise time and time again how you will be up against other professionals who have prepared and that you must work hard for your auditions. I honestly don't know whether this technique will ever work again (remember? You can't predict anything about learning to act.) but it sure as hell is a lot more fun.

The reason that I'm going through these examples is not to remind myself that it's all worthwhile and that I should keep going (well, actually, it is a little bit) but to show that this will happen for you too, if you give it long enough. There is nothing special about me, and I had no signs to indicate that I would be able to achieve these things when I was starting out. Indeed if I had known that I would get to where I am now, it would not have been so difficult to find the motivation to keep going.

So I promise you that the things that you currently find daunting and impossible will happen for you one day. But I'm not promising

AN ACTOR'S LIFE FOR ME

you when. That's the rub. If you stick with acting for long enough, you'll be amazed by what you can achieve, but I can't tell you when that will be. It could be tomorrow, next month, next year or even ten years.

This is why I am now so pleased by the boxes plan that I drew out for you above. It helps me to understand, in a reward-chart type way, that my career is going somewhere, even if the results aren't immediately visible. It really reassures me to think that even if I haven't achieved my career dream right now, at least I know I have ticked off a box and that boxes lead to good things.

There is another timescale consideration. If, like me, you are attempting to learn to act without going to drama school, you have three years' grace! If you had spent that time on a degree, you would not be earning any professional credits or failing at any auditions. In fact, if you consider it properly given that you are (almost definitely, like I am) working on your acting part-time, you actually have even longer until you "graduate".

So when I think of myself as a student, only half-way through drama school, I realise that I'm not doing too badly at all. I shouldn't even be out there auditioning yet, and so anything that I achieve is just a bonus.

Now

It seems that all of a sudden mindfulness is everywhere. Meditation has gone from being a fringe activity to an all-purpose health remedy. Mindfulness is cited as being useful for better sleep, calmer thoughts, better ability to deal with stress and even better relationships. You can join classes, work on your own from an app, podcast or video, and even be mindful "on the go" as you go about your daily business.

(Just for clarification – the reason that I use mindfulness and meditation interchangeably is that in the modern context they mean pretty much the same thing. Strictly speaking meditation is a larger group of different techniques and mindfulness is a subset, but it's not that clear cut. If you are looking for a non-religious practice that involves paying attention to what is happening, you can use either term.)

I became interested in meditation about three years ago. I downloaded one of the most popular apps, Headspace, and had a go at their first ten days. I found it interesting and frustrating. I was a busy person and I found it difficult to schedule in even ten minutes to make it through the daily exercise. I did one exercise, then another. Then I had a gap for a few weeks. Then I did the third exercise. Then I forget all about it and started from the beginning again a few months later. I felt that I really got my money's worth from the ten free audio sessions!

I only started meditation as a regular practice about twelve months after I first became interested. Based on talking to other people, I think that this is quite normal. For significant changes to work their way into your life it takes time. Also just because something doesn't stick right away, that doesn't mean that you won't eventually take it up.

I was on a holiday in Greece when I first started practising meditation every day. My husband was teaching backgammon so

I was free every day. It is much easier to schedule in ten minutes (sometimes even twice!) when you have nothing else on that day. It was also lovely to finish the meditation session and open my eyes to see the wide expanse of the sea in front of me. It felt very zen.

What really got me into meditation was a particular book that I started reading while on this Grecian holiday. The book is called "Mindfulness: Finding peace in a frantic world". It's a great general introduction to mindfulness and it also has a particular slant that I found very illuminating. The authors of the book are key proponents of the mindfulness for depression movement. They work to help people who are having difficulties to use mindfulness to help them to get better.

This means that they explain a lot of concepts in the book that I had not come across before. They talk about how the brain deals with certain types of information, how that leads to depression and how meditation can help you to break out of unhelpful, reinforcing cycles.

This is my favourite example. Your brain works by categorising everything that it comes across. In order to best understand a current challenge, it draws on past experiences that it considers to be similar. Sounds like a great way to do things, right? And yes, this is a really useful way to assess a new chair, by comparing it to previous chairs that you have come across in your life.

But it really falls apart when considering feelings. In order for your brain to consider a sad feeling, it draws up every previous sad feeling that you have ever had, which feels pretty crap. It is also what leads to the feeling that you have when you are sad that you have always felt sad and will never be happy again.

Once you know that your brain works in this way, you have more space and options to decide what to do about it. One of the key themes of meditation is that you need to learn to take your thoughts and feelings less seriously. A way to do that is by realising that you are the observer, so the things that you are able to observe (i.e. your thoughts and feelings) must by definition not be you. They are something that is happening to you.

When I first discovered this, I immediately became intensely curious about certain things that I had been accepting as fact. (Curiosity is another mindset advocated by meditators.) One big "fact" that I have lived with for a long time is that I am mentally incapable of running. I could see that I wasn't physically incapable (although I was sorely tempted to claim that too) but I just hated running so much, I didn't see how I could ever do it. I gave up on it because I accepted my mental state as something fixed and unchanging.

Reading through the descriptions of how we react to things that happen to us – for example the fact that it is often our reaction to the upsetting event, be that pain, fear, betrayal etc. that hurts more and lasts longer – I started to wonder whether this was my problem with running. In general I am not too bad with pain – if I cut myself or similar it doesn't really phase me – the real problem with running is that I have to keep doing the thing that is causing me pain. (Wot?!)

So what if the biggest problem I had with running was my reaction to the pain? What if the thing that I hated most was not the fact that running hurt, but the fact that I hated running? (In a rather circular way.)

Armed with only this idea, and the curiosity to find out whether it was true, I – a confirmed non-runner – set out the following Sunday with my husband and ran 5k. No training, no set up, I just went out and ran 5k. And it did hurt. I collapsed on the floor when I got home. But it proved to me once and for all that what I had suspected was correct. I had more control over my brain that I had realised.

The fact that I had managed to run 5k just by changing how I thought about thinking, gave a big boost to my interest in mindfulness. I started using Headspace (almost) every day. I'm a super-busy person but the convenience of being able to use my phone and only having to commit to 10 minutes every day meant that I could make it work. (And once I was doing ten minutes, they managed to get me to increase up to 15 and then 20 minutes to finish the introductory programme. Of course, I'm back down to 10 minutes now, or five if I'm in a rush.)

Once people knew that I was interested in meditation. I got several recommendations for other apps to try. Calm is a similar app to Headspace. You can use the basic meditations for free and then you need to pay a subscription fee if you want to access the rest of their content. Buddhify is easily the best value app. You pay £3.99 as a one-off purchase fee and then you have access to all of their meditations for ever. The founder of Buddhify has just released a great book on Mindfulness called "This is happening", which I also recommend.

I currently use a mixture of the apps I just mentioned. All of them make reference to walking meditation, which it turns out is as much of a part of the historical mindfulness tradition as sitting meditation. Knowing how to practice walking meditation can make it even easier to fit some mindfulness training into your day. I have a 35 minute walk to work, so if I can't find ten minutes to sit down in the morning, I can always catch up on the way to work.

The more work that I have done in acting and the more I have become part of the acting world, the more I have heard people talk about being in the "now" and saying things like "acting is about responding to the truth of the moment". Mindfulness seems to be exactly what is called for. I have found that my independent study of mindfulness has been one of the most useful tools that I have to hand for acting. It helps in a multitude of ways. First it helps with all of the stress and panic around just deciding to take part in acting.

Yesterday I finished a run of a show. Today I had planned to rest but instead I have had to deal with several difficult emails around a short film that I am co-producing. Learning how much attention I should pay to the voices in my head is super-helpful when I start to feel that all of the acting work I do is "too much" and that perhaps I should just give up and focus on my day job. ("What and I have to write my acting book on top of all this?!")

Becoming an actor is not an easy path. Dealing with your own emotions and criticism and self-limiting behaviour is a big part of the challenge. I have really found that meditation helps with this.

More importantly than using meditation for life challenges, I believe that through meditation you can get a sense of what acting itself really is about.

When I started on stage I had all kinds of voices in my head that would trip me up. (OK, who am I kidding? I still have these. They have just become more advanced and more varied!) There is a constant battle going on in your mind for what to focus on. "The director has told me to stand here.", "I need to be cross, but not too cross." "I am a single mother and my key objective is to protect my child – I must make sure that comes across in this scene".

On top of all that, there is always the worry that I am not dealing with all of these conflicting ideas well enough, that I am simply not good enough at acting, that the director just gave me a note and that must mean that I am rubbish and that I am overanalysing and getting too much in my head and I need to stop all this thinking right now.

There are many different approaches to acting. There are different ways in. Some people use named methods that were expounded by the great actors of the past. Some use a variety of different tools. Despite this I feel that everyone feels the same when acting is going well. (In many ways the tools and techniques are there to help you only when the acting is not going well.) When you are acting well, you are completely "in the moment". You are living the truth of the character.

Meditation is a complex and contradictory discipline. A common instruction is to just watch what is happening, without trying to change it. Let's suppose that you are doing a breath-meditation exercise, where you try to keep your focus just on your breath, for a certain period of time (ten minutes if you are a novice like me!). You will often be advised to just watch what your breath is doing without judging it as good or bad. It is OK if your breath is shallow, or deep, or regular or not. Letting go of judging is a good first step for letting go of trying to change things in order to fix them.

The paradox is that letting go of trying to achieve a certain outcome can often be the best way to achieve that outcome. If you become aware of the tension in your shoulders and accept it as it is, then you will often be surprised to find that the tension has released and your shoulders are relaxed. Contrast that with physically trying to relax when often you simply tense your shoulders into a different position.

This is a great way to explore acting. Rather than trying to "achieve" a certain emotion, or expression or physical response if you are instead aware of what is happening and are able to focus on that, more genuine emotion and responding will often arise.

I did a great exercise around letting emotions arise when I first started working with my coach Jeremy Stockwell. He designated each corner of the room with an emotion – happy, sad, angry and quizzical. I was then instructed to move to the corner that represented the emotion that I was currently feeling.

This was the opposite way round to how I expected the exercise to work. The only way that I had ever thought about acting was to take an emotion and then try to reproduce it. I expected that I would go into a square and then "decide" to become happy, or sad, or angry. This was explicitly forbidden as a way of approaching the exercise.

As I wandered around the different zones, I become more and more confused and bewildered. What was I really feeling anyway? Was I happy? Had my emotion changed? I felt neither happy, sad, angry or quizzical – instead I found a sense of bland blankness inside. As the pressure of expectation to "do well" on the exercise (getting away from trying to "do well" is another thing that meditation can help with) built up, I got so stressed that I just burst into tears.

"Sad corner!" instructed Jeremy.

Being able to sense your emotions and let them out is an important part of acting. In everyday life we are most often encouraged to do the opposite. Rather than realising and accepting that we are sad, we are expected to do exactly the opposite and damp down our emotion. We should not show anyone that we are sad. If you practice this pattern of suppressing emotion for long enough you soon reach the point where you don't really know what you are feeling.

Meditation is a fabulous tool for starting to undo this training that we receive from life. Spending a certain amount of time each day getting in touch with your emotions is part of the first step. I've been learning through coaching that we are not used to sitting with uncomfortable feelings. We find ways to escape them, for example by fiddling with our telephones.

Given how many roles in theatre and film involve being unhappy rather than happy (the happy tends to just come at the end, and possibly also briefly at the start), not being able to sit through uncomfortable feelings is a big issue for an actor. In fact actors often come up with reasons why their characters wouldn't feel so uncomfortable – they try to remove the source of dramatic tension that is causing pain to their character. A good director won't let you get away with that, and if you keep doing it they might try to replace you.

I'm still learning how to best experience uncomfortable feelings. Just being aware that it's something I could do instead of running away is helping. Meditation is all about opening up your mind to see what's really there, rather than what you want to be there.

Interview – Edmund Duff

Edmund Duff has worked on and off as an actor around the country. He is currently an actor based in London.

"I don't think I decided to become an actor, it was something I always did. I was always performing, you know the usual school plays. I didn't think I could do it professionally because I came from a family where it wasn't encouraged. When I was 18, I did an intensive summer school course at the Bristol Old Vic. My dad thought this would burn out the desire to act but instead I wanted to do it even more. I let go of this ambition when my father died. I felt too guilty because my father didn't approve of me acting.

I did amateur dramatics on and off for about ten years. AmDram is full of lovely people but it is just as competitive and bitchy as the professional world. The people I worked with really took themselves seriously. Lots of people who do AmDram are ex-actors or people who went to drama school, but there is a lack of professionalism. Overall the experience was disheartening. It's hard to challenge yourself.

When I was living in Brighton I went on another workshop at ACT in Brighton, which had just started. This made me realise 'I still am an actor' and I decided that I would get on and do it and get professional training. I went to ALRA in London. I chose ALRA because my year was the last year to be auditioned by the founder, Sorrell Carson. She had worked with Joan Littlewood in the sixties; she was very eccentric and had a little dog. She sold ALRA wonderfully to me and also ALRA was one of only a couple of drama schools that offered equal consideration to all mediums.

Training on the three year course at ALRA was intensive. While I was still there I was offered a part on the Discovery channel and so I took the plunge and quit after 2 years to take the part rather than finishing the course. I haven't regretted this decision at all – I started doing things rather than training – but I have used the two years training that I did. There are two types of drama school, nurturing and encouraging ones or ones that flog you and demean you. ALRA was a mixture of both depending on the tutor. Sometimes being undermined by the teacher precipitated a big learning lesson, and coming back to it later it was a big realisation.

I only acted for about a year after drama school. I did a lot of 'walk-on' parts. I felt like my career was going nowhere. I didn't make a conscious decision not to act, it was just that another opportunity came up (teaching guitar in a school and playing in bands). I had an agent but we had a big row and my agent threw me out of his office. My agent didn't seem to care about me at all – he was constantly forgetting what he had put me up for. This added to my bad impression of the industry.

When I moved back to London a friend wanted to make a film about Julia Margaret Cameron (she was a Victorian photographer) and the actor who was playing the role of the husband dropped out. My friend said 'You used to act Edmund'. The director was Peter Dunne and he was putting on a play at the Barons Court Theatre - 'The Communion of Lilies' about Oscar Wilde. Having seen me as the husband of Julia Margaret Cameron, he cast me in the play. It was my first professional theatre engagement for a while. I got the bug and my life had changed again so I felt I could now give it a go. I did a one year course at City Lit, (although it was not a great experience I think it taught me to be resilient and it gave me the foundations to further build upon and ultimately move forward as an actor), and got an agent.

In the 2-3 years since then I've worked a lot, but it's been from roles that I got myself rather than from my agent. It's not my agent's fault – they've submitted me for loads of roles but there is just stiff competition. I've got work myself by working on friends' projects, making contacts through the Actors Centre and applying directly on casting websites (mainly Casting Call Pro). 90% of everything I ever did from day one was through people I knew. But you won't get an audition for Eastenders that way so you need an agent.

You've got to try to forget about yourself and your ego, (i.e. what people are going to think of you) and make your character real and believable. You only get this by committing to the character. You have to not worry, while still being serious about what you're doing.

My advice is to do something to scratch the itch; don't ignore it. Otherwise it will eat you up. If you want to act, act. If you want to be a professional, make sure you have something else to pay the bills! It helps to have some support and people behind you.

In the film K-Pax, Kevin Spacey is an alien in a psychiatric hospital. He eats a banana with the skin on. I did that as an exercise in a class once and vomited. Hats off to Kevin Spacey."

COMMUNITY

Acting is often spoken about as a large family and a community. This is a great way to think about it.

In the modern world we can get too caught up with achievements and industry and trying to work out whether we are doing OK and whether we are up to scratch. You will meet some people like this in the acting world. You can't get away from that. But you can choose whether you want to spend your time with them and whether you want to emulate them. If you choose instead to find the people who view acting as a community open to everyone, I suspect that you will enjoy yourself a lot more, and you will quickly find that you do belong, whatever your current level of experience and skill.

It's important to remember that you choose your community. When you are starting out you might feel that you need to meet the important people who can affect your career – agents, directors and casting directors. Moreover, you will often be encouraged to do this to "get ahead" in your career.

When you get caught up in trying to impress people, you often lose sight of who you really are and what you what. It can be great to learn new ways of acting from a director, but if you focus too exclusively on trying to please them and take everything they say as literal truth, you may not only let yourself become very miserable but also make your acting worse!

Everyone is trying to communicate their version of the truth. That's all that they have access to. Just because someone has become a director of a play, they are not infallible. Even if they are a well-established director, who puts on amazing plays, they are not infallible.

It's worth remembering that when you are starting out, you are more likely to be working with directors who are not as experienced. They will be trying their best to put on a great play, of course, but that doesn't mean that they will get everything right. The trick is to try to not take what they say too seriously, especially if you are tempted to take it personally. At the same time you need to respect that they are the director. They are the only person who can see the show from the "outside" and that they need to be able to co-ordinate everyone together in order to create a finished production.

The part about not taking things personally is really hard to do, but incredibly useful whenever you can manage it. Even if you simply reduce (rather than eliminate) how personally you take something that can be useful. Everyone is dealing with their own demons. They have their own worries and history and insecurities.

People pick up on the smallest of facial gestures. It's obviously not true that everyone knows what you're thinking all the time, but if you are worried by what someone says they will likely pick up on it and worry back, especially if they are inexperienced. So be kind always. Take the positive interpretation of what someone says, and look for ways to help them out without feeling the need to knock yourself out to achieve exactly what they say. Direction is best when you take and interpret instructions rather than implement them to the letter.

I expect whenever you have worked on a theatre show or film production you have felt this sense of community. Suddenly you are all working together to achieve the same thing, in a close-knit and high emotion environment. This sense of community is one of the things that a lot of people love best about theatre and film.

There is also a wider community of actors. I want to mention this because I think we all walk a fine line between – "Oh great! An actor! They will understand what I'm going through." and "Hmm, an actor. What have they done recently? Oh a feature? How did they get that? And who are they talking to? Oh chatting up a director, no wonder they get the parts."

It's really easy to feel like a horse in a race, where all the other actors are running towards the finish line a little faster than you. It can be hard to see other people getting roles and opportunities; it very often feels that by taking those opportunities, they have closed them off for you.

If you do a lot of auditions this can be a particularly acute feeling. At an audition you are literally being lined up again other actors, who often look very similar to you (since you have been asked to audition for the same part). The temptation is to look around, work out what everyone's strengths and weaknesses are (in your head of course, which will almost definitely bear little relation to real life).

You can get used to thinking "She has a great figure" or "He has a very expressive face", comparing yourself negatively to their great qualities. In the same way as trying to take the positive approach when interpreting what a director says, it can also be helpful to stop trying to compare yourself to actors in other ways. There are lots of good reasons for this.

An extremely simple reason is that comparing yourself to other people will make you miserable. Being miserable is bad in itself but – even worse! – being miserable will make you worse at acting. You'll be focussed on the wrong things, not living in the moment and playing a character who whatever their other qualities also has a subtext of jealousy.

Even if you are up against another actor right now in an audition, this is only one job and your life and career are very long. Today's competitor can be tomorrow's collaborator. I frequently need to cast or recommend actors and so I naturally go to those that I have worked with before, even if that just means that we attended an audition together.

(Note that I have also found that being overly friendly to other actors in auditions can put me off my game slightly. Be polite and friendly and focus on what you're there to do!)

Like with most things in life, you can get more out of the world if you can see it as a place where there is a lot of stuff for everyone (i.e. "more fish in the sea" in terms of roles) rather than as one where someone else's gain is your loss. This is called having an abundance rather than a scarcity mindset.

The great thing about having an abundance mindset is that it opens you up to potential opportunities. If you are thinking in terms of competition and scarcity, you tend to shut yourself down. You want to hide any secrets from potential adversaries and you want to maintain your competitive advantage.

If you can open yourself up to other actors and not be scared, you will find that this leads on to more opportunity. For example if you have an audition coming up for a role, and you're happy to chat about this, it might mean that someone thinks of you for another role when they are looking to cast.

I'm not saying that all people are trustworthy, but if you make the first move you'll be surprised to find that more people are than you expected. It's worth being selective to find the right kind of people who trust you back and want to help each other out.

The most important reason to not compare yourself to other people is that how well you will do in your career and how many of your goals you achieve is going to be entirely unrelated to any of the things that you are comparing yourself on. It's a common complaint in the world of acting that talent is not recognised – everyone can point to famous actors who can't act as well as they can.

So at any point in your career you don't know what of your own current skills could suddenly become an advantage, or when you will suddenly "get" the thing that has been blocking you. This is entirely independent of what and how someone else is doing.

(I know that this is hard. This chapter is partly a pep-talk to myself to stop comparing myself unfavourably with people who have been to drama school, trained for many years, worked in prestigious productions etc. etc. But I know it will be helpful if I can crack it!)

Viewing other people as potential collaborators really comes into its own if you are also taking the initiative and creating your own projects. If we are all originating work as well as just trying to be cast in it, you and I are not in competition. In the new artistic economy, the more people making more projects, the better for everyone. As I become an initiator, rather than a follower I am creating opportunities for others. I need actors to be part of my projects. I need actors to collaborate with. I need actors to hang out with.

If you can see acting as a world of infinite opportunity (the new way) versus limited roles (the old way), you will have more fun, develop better skills and ultimately, I believe, become more successful.

Interview – Chris Diacopoulos

Chris Diacopoulos is an actor, director and the founder of the Little Goblin Theatre Company.

"I was always destined to entertain one way or another. That's in my nature. By sheer luck when I was about 11 or 12 my music teacher had connections with Royal Opera House Covent Garden and sent us for auditions for child roles. That's where I did my first professional gig – on the stage of Covent Garden. I walked off-stage saying 'This is what I want to do.'.

In those days when the world was black & white and ran on steam, there were no mobile phones or internet. It was coin-box phone and letter-writing. I remember my end of school career interview. I said I wanted to be an actor and they suggested I work in the army or John Lewis. They had no idea how to be an actor.

I found Spotlight and drama schools. There were only half a dozen drama schools in those days. I got accepted but I couldn't afford to go. It was just as expensive as it is now. A friend of mine mentioned that he ran a small repertory company so I went to audition for him and got the last dregs of rep doing town halls, community halls and small theatres in London and the Home Counties. I worked 4-6 months a year. That was how I was taught to act. It was hands on experience, you got it right or you got shouted at. But you learnt, you learnt about costumes and lights and script. You learnt how to put the show together. Learning from other actors may be harsher than drama school, there is no support mechanism, but you realised that you could actually do it. There was very little money but you earnt a subsistence and you learned. I did this on and off for three years until the company ran out of money.

You had to be an Equity member in those days. The local Equity fixer would come round and check your paperwork/ticket. They were known to close down shows. I had got a half-ticket from panto, and managed to convert it to become a full Equity member.

After a few years of acting and music I decided that it was fun but it wasn't going to happen for me. It was great in your 20s to do sex, drugs and rock and roll, but I wasn't getting the acting jobs and music gigs so I saw it as an enjoyable episode in my life and I went off to be a respectable member of society. I'd been studying martial arts and I became a fight director.

In 1984 the breaking of the unions took away Equity's control of theatre. More drama schools sprung up. My daughter was studying drama and they were doing a version of Clockwork Orange and needed a fight director so I did fights for them. One of the actors broke his leg playing football. I took over the part and that rekindled the urge. Once you've got the acting bug it doesn't go away.

So I came back into the business. I started applying for things and I went back to summer school. I got an agent and got back into the business just to satisfy myself that I could do it.

One thing led to another. In conversation with another actor I had an idea for A Midsummer Night's Dream that I wanted to direct and we put a company together, and toured AMSND around four places. And I realised that was what I wanted to do. I got more directing work. I directed showcases at the Jermyn St Theatre and a couple of other places. Someone else had a play and we did it at the Gatehouse and took it to Bournemouth and it went on from there.

The difference that we find now is that actors are not trained for theatre in the way that we were trained for theatre. They're trained for film & TV. They come in and audition but you almost have to school them again on stage so they can perform to a live audience.

We have to train them in stagecraft, bodycraft, vocal craft, understanding the theatre text and how you perform a theatre text slightly different from to a camera. I believe if you have trained in theatre it is easier to change over than it is the other way round. A lot of the good actors you see on film or TV, you often find that they have theatre behind them. If you walk on stage whether you've been doing it 10 minutes or 30 years you should always be learning something. There is always something there for you to learn. And that's how you build your craft.

The most obvious trait that you need to be a successful actor is a modicum of talent. You can't teach someone to act, you can only help them to act. It has to be in your DNA. I mean to be able to act properly, not to work as an extra. If you're going to play Richard III or Cleopatra you have to be able to do it. You need a deep down spark that allows you to communicate your inner thoughts, emotions and state to the room.

Good actors don't have an ego that they throw around. They are fastidious about what they do on stage, but they don't question what they do and they will always want to do better. They become great actors, and interesting actors. You have to be a very strange human being to want to put yourself through what you have to go through to be an actor. There is a perverse enjoyment in it and you have to be slightly deranged. Lots of people fall by the wayside because the nervousness, the wanting every night to try to do something perfect and to mentally/physically/emotionally bare yourself on stage – it's slightly strange.

Tips for starting out: don't. Think very carefully before you spend £10-12k/year on drama school and think you'll walk out and be a star. If you do it, find something else you enjoy doing at the same time. I got into Aikido and I could always do that and enjoy it. Find something so that when you're not getting acting work you have something else that you love.

The business is about who you know. It used to be about the work, and it should be about the work. If you're performing to thirty people in a small venue it should be about the work, the performance – making those 30 people tell another 30 people how their experience was enhanced by seeing this play. Whereas people instead are thinking who's in the audience and am I going to get picked up for something else. If you think of everything as a stepping stone, you'll never get any fulfilment from it. The last play I did, we all had a fantastic time and did a fantastic show and you just wish everything could be like that. You do it to have a fantastic experience.

I don't even have an agent any more. I walked away from my agent two years ago because what's the point? I'm not going to get picked up aged 60. I do my own work and apply for my own work. Where do the agents get their work from? Just from Spotlight. I can do that myself! If you get a good agent with the right connections with the five Casting Directors that work for the BBC, it's worth it but not otherwise. It's still the old system. Casting for big projects goes to five casting directors, they go to the five agencies that they work with. They only start going outside if that doesn't get someone. It's the same, same system."

FAITH

Faith was not a word that I used often in my life before I started acting. In my mind faith was simply another term for religion, and I wasn't religious. So I rarely spoke about faith and when I did, I expect was quite dismissive of the concept. I had a scientific background and I had found a career where I was looking for the exact right answer. I'd been trained in this way of thinking by years and years of studying mathematics and then working with computers.

Once I started acting, faith became one of those words that started to crop up time and time again. In the first instance, it formed a central part of the Artist's Way which somehow managed to interest me in considering other possibilities despite my fervently atheist background. Julia Cameron insisted that our creative gifts came from outside of us. In her world view God not only created our talents, but required us to use them to give back to the universe.

To start with this whole concept jarred gratingly against me. It felt wishy-washy and, worse, slightly seductive like I was being reeled in to something so that I could be taken advantage of. I latched on to Julia's exhortation that I need not think of God as a religious concept, I could instead think of the universe of the "great creator". This worked well until exercise 1: write a prayer to the great creator. This was definitely religion!

As I carried on with the book, I didn't get more religious, but I did start to understand why this "great creator" was so central to Julia Cameron's world view. Creativity (and I include acting in this) comes from a different part of your brain to rationality. Rational discourse takes concepts and defines and refines them, and fights them against each other to get to the truth. In my common modus operandi I would start with the concept of "great creator" work out what it could and could not be, and conclude that it wasn't "true".

But creative truth (which I now believe is a much deeper form of truth than rationality) does not work along these lines. People who work in any creative field will tell you that their creative buzz gets killed when you start applying rationality to it. Rationality works by reducing the space you are looking at through deduction, creativity works to expand the space you are considering. Rationality is built up cumulatively from what you know, whereas creativity is about taking a leap into the unknown.

Once I was able to accept that creativity worked in a different way, everything became much easier. What if instead of trying to work out whether something was right, or "worth doing" (I spent a lot of time when I was younger trying to work out whether something was worth the effort), you could instead focus on how to make yourself best able to do the job?

Acting works like this. If you spend too long trying to work out whether you are good enough, you will never get started. And you will never satisfy yourself anyway. Actors who have been extremely successful still worry about whether they "still have it" and where the next role is coming from.

Being positive about what you can do and achieve and trying things out works a lot better. This is where the great creator really helps. One quote that really stuck with me from The Artists Way is this: "Creativity is God's gift to you. Using your creativity is your gift back to God." There is a strong sense of obligation to create that runs through the whole book. What better motivator for getting on and doing it, regardless of how good you think you are?

Finding a way to access this mindset is particularly useful when you start out. I'm pleased that I have the opportunity to write this book now, as my eighteen months' experience means that I'm already starting to forget just how super tough it was to decide to keep going when I first started out. I worry that within three years I'll become someone who says "well why wouldn't you just do it?" without an understanding of how daunting it can be.

Acting is a world that is full of gateways with people trying to get you to prove yourself by jumping through various hoops. If you're anything like me, this will make you feel bad. It made me feel bad. I remember feeling that just in order to train as an actor, I needed to already have trained – I needed to have proven myself worthy to take part somehow.

It can feel like a closed shop – if you are a member of Equity, you can become a member of Spotlight. If you are on Spotlight you can join the Actors Centre. If you're not a member of anything already, you need to prove that you have four professional credits. But how can I get the credits until I've been allowed in to train?

I felt like I had all kinds of hurdles to overcome before I could even start learning to act. I felt hopeless, inadequate and like I was in the wrong place. I think if I hadn't had this sense of faith given to me by having read the Artist's Way I couldn't possibly have kept going. Any way in which I could analyse whether I "should" be doing acting, very strongly told me that I shouldn't.

There were some lovely signs that I could spot if I looked very hard. I knew to look for these because the Artist's Way told me that they would be there. If you can have faith in your path, and you let go of trying to analyse and judge, you will find the small signs that you are doing the right thing. Remember that conversely, there is no such thing as a sign that you are doing the wrong thing – if someone is dismissive of you or rude to you, that's on them.

In my first class at City Lit, I felt nervous and out of place. I was pushed way out of my comfort zone by being asked to speak in Gramolo. This is where you talk in mumbo-jumbo as if you are speaking a foreign language. I find it fantastically difficult. I kept going with the class and tried to do my best. At the end of the class, the teacher smiled at me and gave me a piece of Shakespeare to read when everyone else got something modern and unappetising. That was a sign.

I went to breakfast meet up for women in tech that I didn't want to go to. It was early and I could have had a lie in, but I'd said I was going. At that meet up I met a lady who had moved from theatre into tech and who recommended Jeremy Stockwell to me. Jeremy has helped me immeasurably as my coach and has directed two of the plays that I produced.

At the end of 2015 I was offered a one-night run for a production of Tracey Sinclair's Bystanders at the Tristan Bates Theatre. We needed a full two week rehearsal period, and we could never hope to recoup the considerable costs of staging the play in a single night. I nearly turn it down, but reasoned that opportunities were hard to come by and so I should take it. Within two weeks of accepting the single date at the Tristan Bates, I had been offered another week run for the play at the White Bear in Kennington. If I had turned down the production I would have turned down one night, but by accepting it I accepted seven nights across two theatres!

"Leap, and the net shall appear"

"Take one step towards the universe, the universe will take 100 steps towards you"

Faith led me to put myself out there for my first one-woman show, with no idea how I would write it, who would direct it or where it would play. By setting out – by leaping – the net did indeed appear: first in the form of a novelist friend who let me use her character and her story, then by the Actors Centre offering a venue and finally by another friend recommending a director who specialises in one woman shows.

It also worked with the first short film that I produced, although the timescales were longer. The journey of Symptoms is a great example of how sometimes you can't force the outcome that you want – you just need to put it out there and see what happens. I met a screenwriter at a networking dinner and managed to get an option on a short script – all the while entirely oblivious to how good he was. It turned out that the writer, Chris Brown, has in fact won awards for feature screenplays. It's probably just as well I didn't know that at the time otherwise I'd have been too scared to put in my cheeky request for a script he might have "lying around".

I wanted to produce this film so that I could play the lead, which was a challenging role that was way out of my competency. I started to plan the project in the same way that I had with the one woman show – by putting word around that I wanted a director to collaborate with. I very quickly found a co-producer, which was very welcome as I had no experience of film producing (except watching other people do it while I was on set!). He recommended a director he has worked with before and I thought we were set.

Then the director said he wanted to do a test of the scene to check whether I could portray the role as he would like it. Eeek! I was very nervous, but I agreed as I thought he had a right to ask this. So I kind of ended up auditioning for my own film. It didn't go very well. I was nervous all the way through. The director could give me help on what he wanted to see from me, but wasn't able to tell me how to access it. My co-producer, who is also an actor, tried to help – but just seeing that he could act it better than me didn't make me feel any better (quite the opposite)!

So having had my confidence knocked a bit, I shelved the project for a while. My co-producer went on to other things and I bolstered my self-esteem by explaining that I didn't want to work with the director because he didn't have enough experience to get the best performance out of me. Then I let it lie for a while.

When I started to feel a bit bolder, I thought through what I said and got in touch with a director that I had worked with previously on a training course. He would surely be happy to help me work on the character rather than just testing me and leaving me? This was a fabulous development as getting in touch and chatting through things led to another project getting off the ground. But not to a director for Symptoms. I was back to square one and I shelved the project again.

The project started up again when I saw a post on Shooting People. "Does anyone have any scripts?" the post read. "I am looking for dramas to direct." I had a great script lying around – Symptoms – so I replied to the poster and so met Marianna Dean, a fabulous up-and-coming director. She had received tens of scripts and was having trouble finding time to read them all. Symptoms really resonated with her and so we got in touch and started planning.

From that point on we met loads of amazing collaborators, who seemed to volunteer themselves just as we needed them. Fantastic stills photographer Laura Radford posted that she was keen to get involved with short films. We met up with the writer who suggested we would need another producer and lo and behold, the great Ollie Watts posted on Shooting People that he had some spare time to help out producing other people's projects. Ollie knew an Art Director, who came on board (we were lucky as he was booked for another shoot, which was cancelled at the last minute!). I remembered that I'd met an award-winning poster designer and he agreed to help out.

The project came together and succeeded because we put ourselves out there and trusted that it would.

I had had a big crisis of confidence after I was rejected by the initial director. Looking through the consequences of that rejection, however, I think that was the key piece that made the film work. My experience and skill in acting is increasing all the time (and long may it continue to do so!). If I had shot the film 6-12 months earlier I would have done a poorer job on set, even simply through having less experience and being more nervous. Looking back it all seems like it neatly fell into place, and I wish I could have explained that to the twelve-months-previously me who sat crying after the rejection, feeling like I could never be good enough.

This is a great example of how faith helps with the acting journey, how it can help you to book jobs and get projects made and find opportunities. But for me faith goes beyond this. I think faith is integral to the acting process itself.

Acting is a tricky business. I've read many definitions of what acting is, and isn't. One message that always comes up is that as actors we are always learning, which perhaps means that it can't help but always be ill-defined. One thing that everyone agrees is an essential part of acting is portraying emotions that all "normal" people keep safely tucked away and only share with their close family (if then!). When we go to see a play or watch a film, we enjoy the thrill of seeing people in dramatic situations. In order for this to be realistic and believable that means that the actors must be able to appear the same way that they would in those situations.

I have just finished playing a sadistic mental health warder in a play adapted from a Chekhov short story. This has been one of the most difficult roles I have ever played. Like most people, I have spent all of my life cultivating an affable personality and I've worked hard to find out how to make people like me and how to avoid upsetting them. In order to convey the meaning and message of the play I needed to find a way to let that go and to interact with the other actors in the play as if I considered them sub-human and not worthy of respect. This is extremely hard.

It's interesting to note the various ways that my brain tried to get out of properly playing this role. The first way was to not commit. "Perhaps Katya is not really as mean as she is scripted." The second is to break character every so often – to let the "real you" out and so people can see that you're just pretending. The final one is most interesting though. By over-acting the part and becoming a kind of caricature I also avoided showing the thing that was scary and exposing – me being genuinely mean to people.

The most tricky part is that if you are well trained in being a socially acceptable human being, these tendencies have become innate. It's not that I deliberately think "ooh, this is unpleasant", it's that I automatically shut down the natural response.

I feel that my journey learning to act over the last two years has been very much a journey of working out how to let go of these learned responses. I've needed to come away from the emotional safeguards that I've built up to be able to act at all.

This is where faith comes in. We like to do things from a place of knowing. We like safety and security and knowing what's coming.

Acting is about accessing the unknowing. It is relatively easy to put on a copy of a cross expression. It is much harder to let go of trying to create any emotion and live truthfully within the fiction. You need to be able to trust that you won't get hurt, that people won't hate you and that it's all going to end up being worthwhile. Or you have to trust that perhaps you won't get any of the safeguards but that in the end it will all be OK anyway.

I have found some psychological props that I have created to help me. They work a bit like stabilisers on a bicycle. I very often start something by saying "I don't do acting". I find that reassuring. By taking away the pressure to produce something, I find it easier to allow myself to let go and see what is naturally created.

I refuse to do various other things too – character, accents, deliberate emotions. "I don't do emotions" is one of my favourite mantras to myself. By limiting down what I am focussing on to living in the truth of the moment, I avoid confusing myself by adding in unnecessary baggage.

Interview – Peta Lily

Peta Lily is an actor, performer, theatre-maker and director. She has developed a body of Dark Clown work and continues to research this area.

"Although I use acting in my work I tend to call myself a performer/ theatre-maker rather than an actor. I have not followed a typical industry path. The word 'career' sounds like it has some kind of planning or orthodoxy to it. I have come to feel that it may be more useful to think instead of having a 'practice'.

In the very beginning, I only had a clear idea of what I did not want to do. Before the physical theatre movement of the 80's there was little precedent in the UK for theatre encompassing both acting and movement.

I was lucky to have had a few key 'accidents' or turning points which led me to making work (what is now called devising).

I began acting in a semi-professional repertory company in my native Australia, and was fortunate to play roles such as Juliet, Kate Hardcastle and Shen Te/Shui Tah (The Good Person of Szechuan). I also got to perform in Beckett's Act Without Words and in a play called Captain Midnight (done in an ensemble style) directed by Linzee Smith of the innovative Pram Factory Theatre in Melbourne.

An accident of chance brought me to London and, not long after my arrival, I met one day on the Kings Road, again by chance, an actor I had known in Australia, and she recommended I go to Mime teacher Desmond Jones. I had studied dance when young and my attention was captured when I realized that my enjoyment of movement could be brought into performance other than dance. Mime provided an intersection between gesture, expression and emotion. I attended a weekend course, then evening classes – and then committed to a school of Mime.

Here I met two other women with whom, after graduation, I set out to explore and adapt the form beyond the influential style of Marcel Marceau and his 'everyman' character. We wanted to see what female concerns we could interpret and explore. We became a successful Fringe touring company, winning an award at the Edinburgh Fringe Festival, performing in the London International Mime Festival (1981 and 1982) and touring Arts Centres up and down the UK and on British Council tours to Europe. We once made it onto the cover of Time Out.

After three years, I was inspired to move way from shows consisting of several short pieces, and to create longer, solo works. I broke or bent the rules: I added text to mime and dance. My 1984 show Hiroshima Mon Amour (no relation to the film) was a character monologue. Years later, I experimented with two-handed shows in Low Fidelity (a kind of re-invented farce) and the film-language-inspired Beg with its blood-soaked climax (thank you maverick director David Glass and thank you Kensington Gore).

Before the term Physical Theatre was coined, I described my work as Mime Theatre. I worked with no set or a highly minimal set, enjoying the way the form enlisted the physical commitment of the performer, and feeling that it also (when done well) enriched the audience's experience as they invested their imagination in fleshing out the world of the show.

The privilege of being a theatre-maker means you can challenge yourself with roles you might not get to play in mainstream theatre. You can also work from themes underrepresented in the mainstream.

As a performer, what I enjoy are the opportunities to live inside another reality, or to hold the position of guiding an audience through a story, argument or emotional journey – whilst relishing and managing all the technical specificities underneath. It's a feeling of being fully present – occupied emotionally and imaginatively – in flow and engaged with the audience and each fresh moment.

Studying Clown with Gaulier was a revelation. The man offered principles, guidelines and practices to make performing comedy understandable, repeatable. Investigating the craft of Comedy has brought me great satisfaction and holds my continued curiosity. Inspiration came from other artists' work. I found Butoh Dance compelling – it added an extra dimension of awareness; using imagery and attention to physical flow to create rich psycho-physical landscapes inside the body. My Dark Clown work was born from seeing Pip Simmonds Theatre Group present An die Musik and also owed something to the work of Lumiere and Son's Circus Lumiere.

I was very fortunate to have worked early in my solo work with director Rex Doyle, who had acted in Mike Alfred's company, Shared Experience, and I received a Gulbenkian grant to study Direction with Mike Alfreds. Mike's methodology gives clear practices for both directors and actors. His techniques for playing wants, actions and points of concentration are both liberating and delightfully rigorous – one becomes more and more adept at mining and growing one's understanding of the specific flavours and possibilities of humanity. One can build a richly-layered world that connects one to other performers with agile awareness.

I am grateful to all my teachers – there is not the space to expand on all of them here.

Working with Colin Watkeys and Clare Dowie in their 'Stand-Up Theatre' style showed me a way I could create entertaining autobiographical works. Watkeys and Dowie use a direct audience relationship. I love it: I experienced it watching vaudeville as a child; learned it as a form with Gaulier; and saw the magic wreaked so simply and intimately by Rose English in her early solo shows (where philosophical abstraction met mystery and vaudeville). As devisor/director I have helped a number of performers tell their own stories – something I find both interesting and rewarding.

Since 1983, I have made theatre pieces out of the problems and obsessions in my own life. It's highly fulfilling but not the most commercial strategy (although I have been lucky to receive good critical acclaim for my work).

Speaking from my heart, I will always tell people to follow their compulsions. (I don't know what I would tell them from my head…the classic 'have another string to your bow', perhaps). From my gut I might say: 'Dare to do it! Insist on structures that support culture. Devote yourself to the enlivening power of good storytelling. Humble yourself with the rigorous and generous craft of Comedy. Give others the gift of transforming perceptions.'

The path of acting is one that can really develop a person. Actor training has the potential to create compassionate, self-deprecating, flexible, aware people. Is it a 'good career'? Is it a wise choice? Depends on your criteria and your definition of wisdom.

Advice? Read, read, read. See work, see work, see good work. Go to good workshops. Develop practices that you continue. Work on yourself in lots of different ways – voice, body and imagination: Chi Gung, Dance, Feldenkrais, Laban, personal development. For acting you need strong, flexible inner personal resources.

I have heard respected industry actors say that it is impossible to plan a career. There are highly talented and fortunate actors who come out of drama school and go straight into film or television work. Drama schools (I did not study in one but I have taught in several) offer a structured approach with a spectrum of techniques taught by experienced and knowledgeable people - all of which is valuable to the craft of acting. One huge benefit of drama school is the cultivation of discipline, punctuality and other professional behaviours.

You can see from my 'career path' as described above, that I do believe there are other ways to work, to pursue a practice in theatre. Make sure you are covering all bases if you study freelance: look to inform your voice, body, cultural knowledge, textual analysis; become curious about dramaturgy; develop your strengths; challenge your defaults. You will also need to inform yourself on the 'business' side of show business. Network with other creative people. Carry on being creative in considering what is possible and how to achieve things."

GETTING AN AGENT

Worrying about getting an agent has been a big feature of my acting career from the moment I started. I think my initial plan went: do some classes, audition for things, make a short film, do a one-woman show, have I got an agent yet?, do something, have I got an agent yet?, do something, (repeat).

All of the serious advice that I got on how to progress an acting career involved getting an agent. Not just any old agent either; it's very important to get the right agent. Of course the top agents won't talk to you, so you need to be careful who you pitch at, but it should be a good agent. Just not too good.

You need an agent because all of the best roles go to the top agencies only. Although you can sign up for casting sites and see a subset of the work available, anything for "proper" TV or film only goes through agencies.

Despite the fact that everyone knows you need an agent, it seems to also be the case that no-one is ever happy with their agent. I meet lots of actors with agents, and very few find that the majority of their work comes from their agent. If they want to work, they still have to be prepared to find it themselves.

I left writing this chapter until last so that I could see how the whole "do I have an agent yet?" or not thing pans out. And it was a good thing that I did as I feel that I suddenly see the whole issue with a lot more clarity. I'm now pretty sure that the advice I was given, while perhaps technically correct, was not really helpful. Let me explain how my search for an agent has gone.

Getting an agent is probably the biggest example of needing to prove yourself in acting. There are a set number of agents and hundreds of thousands of actors looking for one. If you are a sensitive soul, which you almost definitely are if you want to be an actor, this can make looking for an agent an extremely emotionally tense activity. I think it's even more soul-destroying than constantly auditioning and not getting cast – at least in an audition you get to show yourself off.

I don't think I started out doing the obvious agent actions, although many people do. I think that's because deep down, I knew how it would go. I had been working as a presenter before I started as an actor and I'd been doing much the same thing in pursuit of that. 1. Find contact details of person who can give you an opportunity. 2. Email. 3. Get no response. 4. Call. 5. They say they will read your email. 6. No response. Etc etc etc.

So while I knew it was "important" to get an agent, I kind of held off from printing out my headshot and sending off letters. (More rules: letters are better than emails, except if the agency says email only, but either way they're unlikely to notice you…). I may have half-heartedly emailed one or two, once I got a showreel. But I didn't hear back.

Then I did a great course called the London Actors Workshop. The London Actors Workshop works like a mini drama school. You do a range of different classes over 12 weeks, ending with a showcase to agents. The founder, actor Jonathan Sigdwick, liked to explain that while there were many courses that teach you how to act, not many explain how to get on in the industry. Step 1 for getting on in the industry? Get an agent.

So one of the things we did at the London Actors Workshop was a group exercise in getting in touch with agents. We split up the list of all the agents in the Spotlight contacts book and each wrote to about ten including headshots and CVs of 4 or 5 actors on the course. Because there was a showcase as part of the course, that gave us something to invite the agents to. (Another rule: agents like to be able to see you perform in something, so you're best off contacting them when you're working. Another reason you can't rely on getting an agent in order to get work!)

Between us we mailed (or emailed if they preferred) every agent in the Spotlight book to invite them to a central London showcase. We had four agents accept, and I think some of those had personal links with some of the actors on the course already.

I would have found this process extremely intimidating, except that I'd just had a bit of a revelation before this. I had produced, acted in, part-devised and sold out my first one-woman show. I'd just got a part in a great amateur production through a friend, and I'd discovered that 48-hour film competitions are a great way to get film experience.

I'd also grown in confidence enough to realise what kind of acting work I did, and didn't, want to do. I was happy to do any drama (especially film) even if it was student film, or unpaid work. I was not at all interested in commercials, music videos, corporate work or, in short, any of the options that pay well.

I'd come to the conclusion that I was doing quite well at finding the kind of work I wanted, and I didn't want the kind of work an agent would want to get me. Maybe I didn't need an agent after all? I joined in with all the letter writing and CV posting, because I was part of a group and we were all doing it together. But I felt that it didn't really matter about the outcome for me.

When it came to the showcase I was nervous, because I was always nervous when I was acting at that time. I wasn't extra nervous because there were agents there. I just tried to chill out and do my best. I was acting in a comedy scene and people laughed. So I was pretty pleased with myself.

I love that I'm writing this after the faith chapter. What do you think happened when I decided I didn't want an agent? I got an email after the show from an agency called RS Management saying that they loved my performance and would like to audition me. They were a co-operative agency, and required that I spend one day a week working in the agency as well as being represented by them. I wasn't sure that I could manage this, but I thought I'd do the audition anyway and see if they wanted me.

The audition went horribly. I was really, really nervous and I find it impossible to do a good audition if I'm very nervous. The two people from the agency didn't seem to want to chat about how a relationship would work, which was disappointing (although maybe they'd just written me off!). It definitely helped that I was no longer desperate to get an agent, as I was upset enough just by not performing my best (and the recriminating questions… "Why audition me if they've seen me perform in a piece and I was good?"). It would have been worse if there'd been a lot riding on it.

That settled me though. I would not have an agent. I was just not the right kind of actor. I would find work, and it would be unpaid and I wouldn't have to do auditions for commercials or music videos or any else I didn't want. This attitude lasted for a good six months. I did a play with an amateur company and then one that I co-produced with another actor. I got a part in a no-budget indie feature film.

Things were going really well for me, without an agent. And for some reason that made me think "maybe I need an agent?". As actors (and as people!), we live with a constant fear that whatever we are doing is not enough and that we are missing out. I'd just recently been given the advice again that I must get an agent and that it is very much worth my time sending off emails to people who are not interested in me and either don't reply at all or send me stock replies.

The plus side of things going well for me is that it increased my confidence, and it made me feel I had something to offer. I worked up the energy to sit down and find 4 or 5 agencies that I felt were a good fit. I drafted personal emails explaining what I did and why I hoped it fitted with what they were looking for.

I got a lovely email back from an agency saying that they didn't have room for me right now but that they liked my stuff and I should stay in touch. When I asked how and what exactly they meant by that, I didn't get a reply. I didn't hear back from any of the others. This was enough to dispirit me and put me off the idea of applying to an agency again. I once again made a firm decision that I wouldn't pursue an agent.

And once again, just as I made the decision an agent got in touch! (It's enough to start making you believe in The Secret!) A new agency has started up in Glasgow and contacted me to ask whether I would be interested in having them represent me. I thought about it a little bit as it's risky to go with a new agency (I have heard stories of people's agents simply up and disappearing) and it's also not ideal that they're based in Glasgow. I took the plunge and they're doing a great job applying for a wider number of roles than I have access to.

One thing that is very apparent to me is that nothing has really changed now that I have an agent. I do love to see when they have applied for roles for me on Casting Call Pro or Spotlight, and to be pleasantly surprised to get an audition, but the bulk of my work does not come from them.

If I want to become better as an actor I am still going to need to find and create my own work.

Interview – Paul Foxcroft

Paul Foxcroft pretends for a living. "I wasn't formally trained; I was trained by wolves."

"I didn't set out to be a performer. I sort of never have. It happened by mistake. About eleven years ago I'd been doing some tech for an improv company in Scotland. I took some of their classes to better understand what they did. Then I started my own improv workshops in Liverpool after I moved there, but it was like a cargo cult, I was just teaching what people had taught me without really understanding it properly.

When I moved back to London a friend asked for fundraising ideas for a little fringe theatre – so I suggested an improv show. She wasn't really listening, so a few days later the artistic director phoned up and offered me a cast to work with. I'd read enough to know to say "Yes"! That's how I met Cariad Lloyd and Sara Pascoe and all kinds of great performers. We were put into a room and told do this show and we sort of learned by doing it.

It became a bigger part of how I lived, then I was offered bits of acting work off the back of it. I gave up my day job 4-5 years ago. I made the decision to give up the normal job basically because I was forced to. I really wanted to do Edinburgh and I couldn't unless I quit, I had some work lined up for Sept/Oct so that seemed enough time to see whether it is viable. I also knew I could fall back on working as crew for events in Nov/Dec if needed, but in the end I didn't need to because I had enough acting and improv work to see me through.

Career highlights are hard because I like all of it. Cariad and I have done a few a runs at the Soho Theatre, West End work is always great. Also we did one of our best shows as part of those runs. Each show's different and so it's always a surprise for me. Cariad and I really like being funny, but our style manages to incorporate other stuff e.g. making the audience gasp, sigh – we've had people gasp and exclaim "No" in response to scenes and that level of audience investment is great.

To anyone who is starting out I say "Yes, do that!". If you know you want to do it there are so many ways that you can go about it. Just do your own stuff is the best advice that I can come up with. All the successful people I know, it happened because they did their own stuff. Work begets work. Even if you're just putting your own night on for monologues, sketch or stand up, do it till it gets good. An actress friend of mine wasn't getting much work, so she started doing monologue nights and then wound up doing monologues at a comedy night and got great feedback. She's now an award winning stand-up and as a direct consequence, doing more acting. It's given her the profile, even in a slightly unrelated field, but that helps her to get work.

A lesson that I keep having to relearn is to respect the value of your own work. It's easy to look at everything as an opportunity, but everything has to be judged on a case by case basis. Your contribution is always valid and valuable and sometimes it's worth giving it away because it's good for you, but sometimes it isn't and it's ok to say no to people. Your respect for your own well-being tells other people how much they should respect you.

The best characteristic is the ability to pretend that you are confident. I don't think anyone really is confident but you have to be able to fake it. You need confidence particularly for rehearsal e.g. so that you can try lots of new stuff and disagree with people if you need to. Listening and emotional intelligence are important – your ability to absorb cues and content from people. Both listening to what's being asked of you but also picking up on nuance and just watching people socially to crib their behavioural tics to use later. A great actor friend of mine is amazing at body language and has predicted three bar fights just from watching how people are holding themselves.

Understand that it's work. I've met people who are coasting through – people with no craft who aren't interested in developing. It's one of those things that you never finish learning. I'm doing vocal classes and much more exercise – you are your instrument and it is well worth tuning up

I do OK in terms of making a living. I'm not living lavishly mind you, and I have months when it's rough, months when it's OK and one or two months when it's amazing. I earn slightly more than I did in my full time job, but then that wasn't a well-paid job either. It's hard but it's good that it's hard, in the same way that a workout should be hard.

If you could possibly do anything else, then do that. Acting is the thing you should only really pursue when there's nothing else that makes sense. Because it can be a hard choice to make, every day, to keep doing it.

There's a point in your career when having an agent is really useful, but it's later in your career than most people seem to think it is. At the start as long as you are happy to join Spotlight and CCP you can do it yourself. People make a mistake of chasing agents before they start their career, it's hard to get the agent interested in your potential rather than in things you've actually done, so you're better off just doing stuff. If you've been doing your own productions the agent will be more interested – you're showing that you can and will work. They can send casting directors to you in performances.

I don't regret not having done acting at drama school. When I realise there is a gap I ask someone and I take a specific class with a recommended tutor.

A useful thing to bear in mind is that success is relative. Work out what success means for you. Don't base how successful you are on how successful your heroes, peers or people younger than you are. Everyone wants different things out of this. Some people get really desperate for certain jobs because they're measuring themselves against someone else, which is never a great idea.

My attitude to auditions is that either I look like the guy they are after or I don't. I just try to get a laugh from everyone in the room (I'm usually auditioning for comedy) and be good to work with. I most often get work when I have been referred on by someone seeing me at something else e.g. another casting.

Fighting the voices inside your head is a constant process. It's like with improv: people are terrified and you need to get them to understand that there are no real risks. It's like that – I named my little voice, it's called Poison. When Poison is saying to me "You can't write, you're not funny", I've got much better at ignoring it or writing to spite it. I can also channel the voice and write it out, then I can rub Poison's nose in it. I recently left a joke in a script which I had stressed over so much which then got a massive laugh and I remember thinking "suck it voice".

I don't think I'd ever want to lose that voice as I find elements of fighting it satisfying. I'm now more comfortable improvising onto a page, or "writing" as some people call it, and I can always go back and fix it later if I feel the need. This is a problem that I see a lot (including in improv classes) people trying to be good "right now". You need to get better – like in Malcolm Gladwell's 10,000 hours theory.

I would say to people starting out in acting – be bad at it for a bit. Enjoy that time. You're supposed to be bad at it. A toddler isn't great at walking when they start out. It's a skill. People think you're either good or not, but if you are willing to be honest about how you are progressing you will get better. The reason that most people give up on writing something is that it's bad, but you should carry on, finish it, go to sleep and edit it in the morning with a fresh approach. Nothing good happens outside the edit.

I've never made it through The Artist's Way. I've started it two or three times, but I'm not great at making a schedule. Julia Cameron's The Artist's Way is a great resource. I do want to make it through the twelve weeks one day. If you want to make art just do it by any means, the only obstacle is yourself. You worry about not being good and people not wanting to look at it, but great artists didn't care about people looking at their stuff, they just did it because they had no other choice".

TALENT

Nature versus nurture is a big debate in all areas of life. It has been going on for a long time – the distinction was originally summed up in this language by none other than the Great Bard, who coined so much of our language – Shakespeare. In The Tempest it is said of Caliban that he is "A devil, a born devil, on whose nature/ Nurture can never stick".

General thinking has moved away significantly from a pure nature argument in recent years. Books such as Outliers by Malcolm Gladwell and Bounce by Matthew Syed point to the main commonality between "geniuses" being the number of hours (approximately 10,000+) that they have dedicated to their expertise.

A common mixed viewpoint is that people are like an undeveloped photograph. You will have nothing of worth if you don't develop the photo correctly – the "talent" will go undiscovered – but similarly you can do all the developing you like but if the picture ("talent") isn't there in the first place it will achieve nothing.

I am a big subscriber to the 10,000 hours view of talent. This is partly because it fits with how I would like to believe the world is. It appeals to my egalitarian viewpoint. I find the concept of innate talent slightly distasteful – it feels like a way of segregating people into those who are "special" and those who are not.

Something else that reinforces my point of view is its practical nature. Lots of work has been done into how people best develop. It turns out that if you believe in talent, which is referred to as having a "fixed" mindset, you don't do as well as if you believe in nurture, i.e. a "growth" mindset. Children who scored well in tests and were told that they were naturally gifted performed much less well in subsequent tests than those who were told that they had succeeded because they had worked hard. Thinking success comes from working hard means that you work harder in the future which leads to more success.

I actually take a slightly stronger view. I don't know whether nature or nurture is more important. But I don't care. Because it's more useful to believe in nurture. There's nothing you can do about nature, and it's really easy to misjudge how good you can be based on how good you are right now. In fact it's impossible – although far from where I'd like to be, I am already immeasurably far from where I was when I started.

The other thing to remember is that how good someone is is not an objective science. I read an immensely good online article on acting written by a film director, in which he talked about what makes a great performance and hence a great actor. He used Keanu Reeves as an example of someone that he didn't personally rate. The director was very diplomatic and said of all of his comments that they were just his opinion, but I think he was spot on with the kind of things he was praising and they matched with a lot of common wisdom around what good acting is. Despite this, all of the comments underneath the article were disagreeing with his assessment of Keanu; talking about how good Keanu Reeves was in the Matrix and how his particular style of acting was well suited for the role. There is no objective truth on what talent is.

In acting, much as in life, being the best version of yourself is a really legitimate goal. There is no objective target for you to hit and no concrete way to grade yourself against other actors. You will do best by focussing on developing what you have, not looking at what you lack.

My father-in-law is a big fan of many of the great figures of history. One day we were having a conversation about Mozart and he challenged me to admit that Mozart was clearly a genius, that Mozart had that "something special" that no-one else had. I don't believe this. Mozart had a very particular upbringing where he was writing symphonies aged 8. While this is commonly used as an indication of his genius, it is also great evidence of the 10,000 hour theory at work. If Mozart started aged 8 (or even earlier) he would have got his 10,000 hours in a good deal earlier than anyone else. By the time he was 12 he would have looked like a prodigy.

I am not prepared to compare my father-in-law, or anyone else who hasn't done as many hours as Mozart to the composer and say that they are less of a genius. I don't believe you can know until you put the hours in.

I recently heard a fantastic phrase that sums this up for me. "People frequently over-estimate what they can achieve in the short term and under-estimate what they can achieve in the long term." So when you are starting out you will be dismayed by how slowly things seem to be going. But if you stick with it you'll be bowled over by how you have changed over five years.

If you want to try and define what acting talent is, then I think there are two main parts to it.

First there is the range of expressiveness that you use as a human being. This changes over time and can be learnt. You are likely to learn some things by virtue of being in new situations in life and having new things to communicate. If you put yourself out there and start public speaking, or get promoted into a new role, you will start to communicate in a new way. If you have a child you will need to put your points differently. You can of course learn things deliberately – the most likely way being through acting or communication courses.

More important than this is whether you are able to reproduce this expressiveness within the fiction. Acting is about looking like a real person in what is essentially a made-up situation. You may find that you are able to transfer some of your natural expression across, but struggle with other parts. For example, once you are adept at public speaking, acting a public speaker is pretty straightforward. But whereas you may be able to convey compassionate sympathy flawlessly to a grieving relative, it may not be so easy when you need to do the same in a film.

My experience to date has shown me that the first of these matters less than you think, especially when you are starting out. There will always be parts that need people just like you, with exactly the responses you have (especially if you write yourself those parts in your own plays or web series!). If you are an introverted, guarded person – that will be needed for some film parts.

The second, on the contrary, is much much harder than you would expect. Imagine if someone said to you – we'd like you to act in a film and you will play yourself. That sounds easy, right? Yet somehow it isn't. Yes, you can get on with whatever you would be doing normally and let someone film you, but that's not what I'm referring to. What if you have to "be you" but there are cameras and lights and you have to say specific words at specific times? And look natural?

I recently finished a one-woman show at the Pleasance Theatre. One of the parts of the show was me demonstrating three different ways to tie my shoelaces. The show was devised by me and the director Jeremy Stockwell in the three weeks preceding the performances. Jeremy was taking me through various questions about "shoes", which was the first topic of the show and we got on to how to tie your shoelaces. I am quite excited about the way that I tie my shoelaces, as I only learnt it a couple of years ago and it's a really neat way to do it. (Grab me at an event sometime and I'll show you….) When I was just answering Jeremy's questions, I could happily, enthusiastically and expressively explain about how to tie my shoelaces.

Then I was asked to do it "on stage". (Where "on stage" simply mean in a designated space in the rehearsal room and as a performance.) Suddenly I became extremely wooden and nervous and had to give up half way through saying "I can't do this". What's that about?

I clearly could do it since I had been doing so just a few moments ago. But put me in the spotlight and it's suddenly a different game. I had to "practice" doing up my shoelaces about four times before I could conceive of acting it the same way that I could do it without the pressure of anyone looking at me.

Over the last eighteen months I've been learning various ways to get better at this. As with everything, practice is certainly a big part of it. As you act simpler and simpler pieces you will start the process by simply learning how it can feel different and that you may get caught out when you feel something is simple to execute.

You can start to try different ways of getting "in the moment". You can create a character back story so that you can fabricate thoughts to have while you are acting. You can focus very intently on what is going on around you. You may also need to investigate ways to feel less stressed and less self-conscious. You will definitely need to learn how to take yourself less seriously!

How well you do at this will determine whether people think that you have talent. If you are nervous when you are acting, that is the most sure-fire way for you to act in such a way that people will dismiss you. I wholeheartedly believe that only if you focus first on how to become less nervous on stage, will you build the solid foundation that you can add techniques, character and emotional range on top of.

Early on in my acting journey, I took a great course for actors of all levels of experience called the London Actors Workshop. Two of the classes were taken by a TV actor called Paul McEwan. Like in many courses Paul worked with each of us to refine our TV acting technique. What was remarkable was that he gave every single actor on the course advice that made their acting instantly more believable. While I was watching everyone else through a camera I could see the change in how they came across. (I hope the same was true for me!!)

At the end of the class Paul was asked when you could tell whether someone had talent or not. He replied that different people develop at different times. He said that he had seen many actors that didn't "get it" for years and years and then suddenly had a breakthrough. He said that for that reason he never wrote off anyone as an actor.

That struck me as a very powerful belief and was, I believe, the underpinning for why he got such great results for everyone on the course. He genuinely believed that they could act, if they could unlock it in the right way, and so he focussed on how to help them do that rather than criticising what they weren't doing right.

You may find that your level of nervousness depends on what part you are playing. I found that even as it became easier for me to relax when playing parts closer to my real life (mid-thirties professional woman), as soon as I was given something more exposing I felt like I was back to square one.

A play that I performed in in 2016 was an adaption of Chekhov's Ward 6, one of his short stories. The play was set in a mental institution, where the patients were neglected and regularly abused. I had to play not a poor, abused patient, but a sadistic nurse who not only shouted at and hit the patients, but also assisted her colleague in raping them. This was way outside of my comfort zone!

On the first rehearsal day, I tiptoed nervously around the set. I was reprimanded several times by the director for being "too polite". I had done only a single stage combat class so I was worried about pretending to hit the patients in case I ended up actually hurting the actors. All in all, I was no good at all.

Three weeks of rehearsals later and I had settled in to the role. I had some techniques for hair pulling and choking people, and now that I felt much safer in terms of not really hurting people I was better able to act viciously. The more of these roles that I have the opportunity to do, the easier it will become to do new and different roles outside of my experiences (I hope!). The more difficult a role is, the more it's stretching you.

Once you get more comfortable doing a wider range of things on stage and film, you have the opportunity to start to develop your technique further and to grow your emotional range. I feel that I'm still a long way from this, but that doesn't mean that I can't get there. If when I first started acting eighteen months ago I'd invested my energies in trying to work out whether I had any talent or not, I wouldn't be here now eighteen months better.

Acting is a skill that you keep learning for the rest of your life. It is a craft that you work on. Whatever stage you are at in that learning is completely OK and it is fine for you to act while being at that stage in your learning. By constantly trying roles that are just outside of your competence you will grow and you will start to stretch yourself.

Stick with acting for two years and you will start to see your talent shine through, wherever you started from.

Interview – Al Carretta

Al Carretta is a theatre and film producer and director.

"I never consciously decided to become an actor; it was a necessity of competition. Even now I refuse to sell myself as an 'actor' per se for one simple reason; as of 2015, I have been afforded the opportunity to perform in a production other than my own only once.

In May 1999, at Keele University, I staged my first original theatre production and concentrated solely on direction. The same Summer I was due to perform in two student drama shows heading to the Edinburgh Fringe. I could see that I was the production's weak link and argued until the 11th hour to be written out of the productions as my contribution was detrimental to the shows at large. Eventually, everyone else grudgingly accepted the points of a moaning upstart and with a matter of days to go things took dynamic shape and culminated in a four star Scotsman review. From here, I began to understand that acting is a much bigger machine than just delivering lines on stage or screen. At core I'm a writer/producer/director, however, my interpretation of this role is to be the figurehead of a project. To manage effectively, you need good people skills. Interpersonal relationships require construction through progressive scenarios. Acting is an application of this knowledge so if you know how to look after people, you know how to react to the potential crises present in any given situation. Having learnt this at 19 from a defining, real world experience, I realised to get the most out of a cast you need at minimum to be on par with them, hence, choice actually becomes a necessity.

Look at the Edinburgh Fringe as a benchmark for the Arts World and you'll see that in 2016 everyone is a comedian, everyone is trying to be funny and few people attempt heavyweight performances, as proven by a simple fact; the theatre section in the guide gets thinner every year.

The change in audience dynamic is huge; not only is it de-sensitised it is uninformed over a previous generation of theatregoers. People haven't grown up with as many classic texts, media discipline is non-existent and with this the style of acting has too because traditionally visual media (and this includes film) cast personalities and theatre cast performers. As of 2016 the mould is broken but not necessarily to the benefit of the 'industry' at large. There are more 'triple threat' performers than ever but fewer emerging character actors.

For a production company, the ability to source talent is easier than ever and casting sites have improved immeasurably in the past 10 years, however, whilst communication protocols change the design remains the same. Acting is a closed shop dominated by nepotism, vanity and shifting palates of commercial taste in body image, style and vocal character.

I don't call this a 'career'. It's something I do because I'm passionate about it but I've just never had the luck, opportunity or group of like minded people around me to step up so until I've earnt £500k and caught up with what I should have generated in terms of income over the years I dismiss this a 'career'.

On the flip, I've put in a gameplan to develop an idea and have delivered everything possible on the resources available. Since inception I've worked on three progressive five year plans. Technically, I'm on the fourth now. I started in 1999 as a theatre company wanting to stage original plays and classic dramas in my local area (Gillingham, Kent) and the Edinburgh Fringe. I transitioned into short film production and venue management then moved into gig promotion and started feature film production. By definition a career should come with opportunities for progress. From my first independent production in April 2001 to Nightpiece Film Festival in August 2015 and shooting 'Bad Caller' in 2016, nothing has actually changed; I'm still doing the same thing, I've still got the same idea I'm just a thousand times more efficient at their execution and I can still do it cheaper than anyone else.

Arguably, going to Keele University and becoming involved with the drama society was a decision that heavily influenced my life but it's my attitude - and this alone - that has made productions happen. I've done so many projects simply for lack of a better idea because I know without something happening you have nothing to go forward with.

I've staged productions to prove a point and challenge opinions of the status quo. How did I get better as a performer? I afforded myself the opportunity to fail. You have to literally book things up and see if they happen. I've been told to stop wasting money on Edinburgh, theatre and films since I started because, with a certain degree of irony, it's actually a total lack of support that cements the point I have reached. Many people will point to a single person or production that is responsible for their (elevated) progress. For me, 1999 was the last and only ever year significant opportunities were offered to me that weren't created by myself. Mentally, you get very hard when you aren't helped - you have to simultaneously maintain faith and give up on people at the same time. You need a social network and a team of people who believe in you and constantly promote your efforts.

Perform under the radar until you have profile then launch yourself fully formed. Question your motivation and understand, without any doubt or apprehension, that the way you sound and the way you look will be the single most defining aspect of your employability is a performer. There is no meritocracy in play in imagination land.

Cultural deprivation is reflected by the ability of any given person to present or consume multiple artistic disciplines at a price point relative to their earning power in a region that can be considered in their vicinity. When accessible art is absent, cultural deprivation prevents establishment or reinforcement of disciplines that positively increase the quality of life in any given community. The ability to participate in a discipline such as acting therefore becomes a hi-culture consideration and a role that is universally accessible in principal but not practice. In a nutshell, acting is a measured choice for the financially prepared but a financial precipice for most."

BUT WHAT IF I'M NOT SUPPOSED TO BE DOING THIS?

It is a common trait of humankind to wonder what we are here for. We want to know what we should be doing and how we are to go about it. Now that the majority of us live above and beyond simply scraping along for a living, we can't help but think about what else we could be achieving and contributing. What does a well lived life look like? What do I want to be able to say about myself on my death bed? Should I focus on helping others and making the world a better place? Should I be finding my unique gifts and sharing them with the world? Or is aiming for any of that getting above my station? Should I just keep my head down and focus on trying to feel grateful for what I have rather than longing for things that I don't have?

All of these questions are unanswered for almost all people. You are not alone if you are wondering this. I've noticed a tendency among really successful actors to say in interviews that they always knew that they wanted to act, that they were drawn to acting and that they couldn't possibly do anything else. If you feel like this, then fabulous, keep going! It will serve you well as you start the long hard journey to improve your acting skills. However the converse is not true. You can be an actor even if you don't feel you were born to do it. You can be an actor just for a bit, for one show, or to see whether you like it or not. You can work at acting and get better at it, then leave it and come back to it. You can have fun with acting. You can be a dilettante. And most importantly of all you can continue to pursue and pour your heart and soul into acting without knowing whether it is what you are supposed to be doing or not. Let's be honest. This is how most of us live our lives. There is no certainty. We change our minds every few seconds about what we should be wearing, let alone what direction our lives should take. That's OK. It is most certainly not a reason to quit. One of the saddest things that I heard was a friend who said that he had always wanted to be a novelist but had been convinced by a quote from Rainer Maria Rilke that unless he had a burning desire that overcame everything else he was clearly not supposed to be a novelist. Not true!

I wanted to take this opportunity to say that I constantly constantly doubt whether I should be investing so much time, money and effort into becoming an actor. Not only when I have a bad show, or a bad review or somehow feel I am not up to scratch, but in a more holistic existential way. Shouldn't I be more passionate about it? Shouldn't I feel that I will die if I don't act? And I am coming to the conclusion that no, I don't need to feel any of this.

I think that the reason that many successful actors say that they always knew they wanted to act is not because that is a pre-requisite for being able to do it. It's not because there is a right type of person and a wrong type of person and that if you were supposed to be an actor you would "just know". It's because coping with doubt is super-hard. Learning how to act is hard enough.

Learning how to deal with your inner critic is even harder. But having to fight through the idea that you might just be wasting your time, and weren't you quite good at accountancy, and aren't there all those other opportunities in the world, and wouldn't life be better if you just chose something where people were nicer to you and everything was easy, that's the hardest of all. So maybe the reason that people who have acquired unassailable faith that THIS IS WHAT THEY'RE SUPPOSED TO BE DOING are more successful is simply that they have one fewer thing to think about.

The Actors Centre have been arranging a series of conversations with well-known, successful actors. It's great to see their perspective, how they got to where they are today and how they struggle too. Yesterday I went to see the incredible Dame Judi Dench. She talked about the need to be positive. This is great advice. It's so easy to try and predict the future, and when you are feeling down you will predict it in a negative way. You'll group all your negative experiences together and predict that everything will fall apart for you. It is easier to keep going if you can focus on concrete, positive things that you can do to make things better. Making your own work and initiating your own projects is a fabulous way to take control. It is one of the most positive things you can do.

Even when you have been positive, and had some successes and started to feel like you are getting the hang of it, something will come and knock you again. It's like a cycle. You get a part, you feel positive, you do a better audition, it becomes a pattern and you see everything through a positive light. You look at how far you've come and what you have achieved. You feel you can draw a graph with an upward trend.

Then the work goes quiet. You don't get any auditions, and when you do you get a suspicion that you lost the role because you were too "in your head" worrying about how you're not very good. You completely lose sight of everything that has happened and instead can only see a mountain to climb ahead of you. You feel like you've been on a plateau for as long as you can remember. Or have you even gone backwards?

When I first started making notes for this book, I noted down that "after one year it doesn't go away". I had been working very hard and feeling too busy, and yet at the same time feeling that I was going nowhere. I felt no further along than I had at the start.

I can confirm, while I am now writing this book, that it doesn't go away after two years either. I am just finishing a really busy quarter, where I did two plays that were both very stretching for me, and several pieces of filming. I have one shoot left to do in a couple of days' time. I am already starting to sink into the panic of "What's coming next?!". Having done all these amazing things in the last three months is scant consolation to me. It seems that it is more energising having things to look forward to than having done them.

This is a key lesson of life. We often think we will finally be happy when we achieve things – possessions or goals or relationships. Acting credits, in this case. Yes, there is a brief euphoria when you get something you want, but it is astonishing how quickly it subsides. I have heard that the worst day of an Olympic medal winner's life is the day after winning Gold. Winning Gold is an incredible feeling – the culmination of all those years and years of effort, a truly significant achievement. But after that rush is gone, what is left to do? The dream is achieved. The motivating force that has got you out of bed every day is gone. You have nothing left to work towards.

This can sometimes help, remembering that "this is the work". This is the job, applying for roles, being rejected, auditioning, getting cut from a series, going to classes, going to more classes, always looking back at your previous tapes and thinking "I could do that better now". I don't have any experience as a Hollywood superstar but while I am sure there are upsides, I am also sure that this basic fact about human nature doesn't go away. There are still projects you want that you don't get. There are still times when you wonder whether you will work again. There are still days when you don't have the energy to get up and do the things you know you have to do.

Something else to throw into the mix, is the little phrase that has become modern culture's favourite acronym. FOMO. Fear of missing out. Ever felt like all the other actors you know have better jobs than you, more work, more opportunities? Does it make you feel sick to read about people's rise to fame? It certainly does for me. I just read an article about how brilliant Meryl Streep was in Kramer vs Kramer and it put me on tilt all morning.

FOMO interferes with my positive planning too. What if I didn't apply for that role, but it turned out to be amazing and with a great director and something that would launch me? What if I didn't open the email full of unpaid jobs from Casting Call Pro but there was a brilliant role in there that was perfect for me that I would definitely have got? I go to auditions rather than resting, I shoot small unpaid parts at immense effort to me when I could have been working on my own video series.

Sadly, the answer is not simply to become more successful. Fear doesn't go away just because you are doing better. In many cases fear increases when you have more to lose. The best approach is to find strategies that allow you to evade FOMO and get on with your own life. Don't read the articles about people who have already made it. Don't compulsively look up the credits of everyone you are playing with. Do congratulate people when great things land for them. (Yes, this advice is all directed at myself!) And when you succumb to FOMO, forgive yourself, eat some chocolate and get back on the horse.

There is an upside to all of this. The key way to improve your acting ability and to develop yourself in general in life is to go out of your comfort zone. Acting an emotionally difficult part is about staying with uncomfortable emotions for longer and more deeply than you usually would. Networking, "selling" yourself to agents and casting directors and producers is always out of your comfort zone.

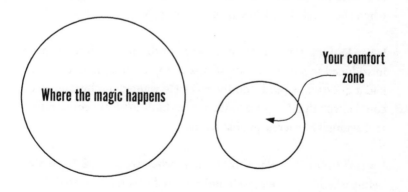

Most people in the world explore and learn the most they ever will in their lives when they are children. As children we are almost always out of our comfort zone. We are always falling over, scuffing our knees and running crying to our parents. As we get older we start to get good at stuff. We "work out what kind of person we are". We start to make a comfortable nest and then suddenly one day we find we are scared to leave it. Many, many people all around the world are successful, comfortable and deeply unhappy.

When you feel this fear of acting, and the process of acting, and the worry that you are not good enough for it – you are out of your comfort zone. This means that you are learning and growing. If you were just acting in things where you felt totally comfortable and confident it would mean that you were stuck and not getting any better.

I experienced this to a great degree when rehearsing for the lead role in a short film about a lady with cancer. In the film she opens up to the doctor and explains how scared she is about the impact of cancer on her life. Her emotional journey, including the point when she bursts into tears, is tightly scripted.

I was looking for a director to work with on this film. I'd been introduced to someone who was keen to do the film, but then he had a question. Could I do the role? He wanted a rehearsal so he could check that I was up to the job and I didn't feel I could refuse as it seemed like a reasonable request.

I wasn't in the best place emotionally when we started. I resented being asked to prove myself and mostly I was really scared that I couldn't do it. All my insecurities backed this up – I didn't have training, I didn't have techniques to use, I'd never done it before.

And it didn't go well. I felt scared and kind of frozen while I was reading. The director would ask for things and I had no idea how to produce them. "I see her with more vulnerability," he said. "You're too controlled." Another actor had come with me to read and he suggested we swap parts so I could see how he did it. He did it great. That didn't make me feel any better.

After trying to get the right performance from this script for a couple of hours, the director suggested we call it a day. I racked my brains for something that could be a solution and suggested I run the lines with my acting coach. We all agreed that would be a sensible next step.

I think it's fair to say that this was the lowest point (so far!) in my acting career. I had thought that I was on the right track. I had been so pleased with myself that I had found a great script and shown enough initiative to get a project moving so that I could act in it. Yet I had been let down by my ability to act. Should I have gone to drama school? Or did it just mean I had no talent?

I went off to see my acting coach as it felt like a positive step I could take. I explained the situation to him and also confided my fears. I felt at that point that I had it all wrong. I wanted someone else to take responsibility for my acting ability and to magically make me good. "Please can I just go to RADA and get my training done for me????"

We worked on the piece and I had a really interesting experience. Getting out of my head and emotionally involved with what was going on was a much better way of getting the "right" emotions that any amount of back story and cancer research. At the end I felt adrift and suddenly very worried about having cancer. "Don't be stupid," said Jeremy. "you're don't have cancer and you never have had." Oh yes.

I realised that as a junior actor I needed a director who could take the time and help me get to the performance in the way that Jeremy had. I saw that I could look on it as a relationship rather than just putting all the blame on myself for not being able to do it. I suggested to the director that I looked for someone else and he agreed. I think he was relieved.

I ended up shelving the short film until I serendipitously met an amazing director about six months ago, and we recently finished production. Looking back now the whole experience can be viewed as a positive part of making the film. I wasn't ready then, and it wasn't the right partnership. By going through the heartbreak of "failing" I allowed myself the opportunity to come back to the project and make an amazing film (touch wood!).

Earlier this year I worked on a one-woman show called "HOW TO DO ACTING (Properly)". The idea was to produce a stage version of this book – a show about my experiences learning to act. Jeremy Stockwell and I devised the show together and the end result is a great combination of my thoughts and theories and Jeremy's ideas and structure. Do go and see it if I get a tour off the ground!

The devising process was very intense. Jeremy would ask me questions, or ask me to do things ("Show me how you tie your shoelaces".), I would do them, Jeremy would give me notes and then we'd see whether they'd fit in the show.

I don't know whether this is a result of the devising process, Jeremy's directing style or whether he was deliberately trying to stretch me, but throughout the whole process I was frequently outside of my comfort zone. From simply trying to tie shoelaces "on stage" in as natural a way as I did when I was just explaining to Jeremy, to talking in Gramolo – improvisation in a made-up language (this was not used in the show as it was so far outside my comfort zone I "couldn't do it"), to drawing free expression pictures on a flipchart, I was constantly growing in what I was able (and prepared) to do.

Whenever you start to feel the fear that it's all too much and you can't carry on, that's the universe telling you that you're doing good. Now I just need to remember that next time I feel like this.

Interview – Yang-May Ooi

Yang-May Ooi is a novelist who went on to perform her first one woman show, Bound Feet Blues for a three week run at Tristan Bates Theatre, Central London.

"I started life as a novelist but I wanted to tell my family story. I wanted to portray Malaysian English but on the page it just looks like bad English. I realised that the stories passed down to me by my mother and grandmother were oral stories so they needed to be told out loud. I tried some live storytelling at Spark London and The Story Party. I could use my British and also my Malaysian voice and the audience loved it.

I signed up for a workshop at the Centre for Solo Performance. I wanted to integrate more physicality into the delivery of my stories. I worked up the script of Bound Feet Blues there. We had a scratch night at Conway Hall and got the chance to do it in the main auditorium. I had no expectation that the piece would go any further. I approached the scratch night as if it was the one and only time I would get the chance to perform Bound Feet Blues. I invited my friends. I designed a flier at the last minute late one night and circulated it online.

Annie Kwan, one of the producers of the South East Asian (SEA) Arts Festival, was googling for East Asian storytellers for the Festival. She came across my information online about the scratch night performance. So she came along to the event.

I had never performed without a mic so I found a voice coach, Jessica Higgs, and had some lessons. Jessica is also a director so she worked with me to extend my emotional range and gave me some guidance on improving my dramatic performance of the script. On the scratch night, the audience was completely mesmerised by the piece - I surprised myself at how powerful my performance was.

Annie Kwan invited me to bring the piece as a theatre production to the SEA Arts Festival. At that point I knew nothing about theatre, and I had no idea how to put on a production. But when someone offers you this incredible opportunity, you just have to say YES!

I asked Jessica if she would be my director and she agreed. I finished the script within the next few weeks. We then had six months to develop it into a theatre piece that was good enough for the professional stage. We worked towards a one-night showcase. Jessica brought in producer Eldarin Yeong and we got some Arts Council funding.

Jessica got me to the level of a professional stage actor in three months. Rather than doing rehearsals for a few weeks before the show, we spread it out over three months - in between, I worked by myself to lock in what came out of the work we did together. The showcase at the Tristan Bates Theatre took place in October 2014 and was sold out months ahead of the night.

Ben Monks, one of the creative producers of the Tristan Bates Theatre came to the showcase and afterwards described it as "a powerful, provocative and intimate story told in an intelligent and engaging manner". He invited us to do a three week run as part of their November 2015 programme.

For me, I wanted to see how far I could take it. A three week run in Central London (West End!) was a once-in-a-lifetime opportunity. This was a unique personal achievement but I don't want to tour the show and I don't want to have the life of an actor.

I loved the rehearsal process but it was stressful. Because I was not professionally trained, I had to learn everything that an actor would learn in three years over a compressed timescale. I had a dramatic and narrative instinct but it needed to be honed into the discipline and stage presence that a professional actor would have. If you go to drama school you learn stage craft and you have the techniques of acting ingrained into you over time. I had the raw talent but Jessica, on top of directing the play, had to train me in all the things that an actor who had been to drama school would have learnt. The control and precision that came from that training and discipline gave my performance its power and impact.

It was a huge confidence boost: standing on stage in theatreland, the star of my own show, an East Asian woman at age 50+, with my grey hair and glasses. I had always thought that to be an actor you had to be beautiful like Juliet Stevenson, and here I was an ordinary person. It felt surreal.

The audience over the three week run was intently absorbed - you could hear a pin drop. We had no props or costume, just the set. I was barefoot and dressed in black. I created the whole story with just my body and voice. The story took place in Oxford, Malaysia, ancient China and the Australian Outback. I had to create everything the audience "saw" out of nothing – including demonstrating foot binding using my left hand as a foot. It was magic.

This is the magic of theatre. You don't need a helicopter arriving and laser light, just the audience's imagination and you.

I am also a professionally qualified coach. Someone commented that since doing the show, I hold myself with a star quality. It is a quality that is hard won. I used to be self-conscious and shy. One of my aims in my coaching work is to encourage others to step into their star quality.

We all have a star quality and it's a question of whether we dare to show it. Particularly for women, we are taught in many cultures to take the supportive role and let other people shine. But by shining ourselves we can set an example for others. It's not an ego thing. It's 'here I am' and I am going to take up my rightful place in the world. Together as women, the more we dare to shine, the more we can take up our place in the world and be powerful."

THE FUTURE

I feel immensely lucky to have the opportunity to write this book at this point in my career. Things have changed so much for me over the past twenty-four months that I can only dimly remember how imposing and terrifying everything was when I started out. I worry that in another twenty-four months I will become one of those jovial people who can't see the negative side of anything and will cheerfully mutter "Well why not just try it dear?" when people come to me paralysed with fear about taking the first step as an actor. I want to look back on this and remember the change that comes when you stick with something and keep trying. I want to know that application and persistence leads to learning and that the feeling of being totally overwhelmed diminishes. I can't help but feel that this is an important life lesson for anything that we set out to do in this world.

I'm proud of where I have got to. I've achieved a massive list of things that I didn't think would be possible: getting accepted onto casting sites and as part of organisations as a "professional" actor, being cast from audition performances, playing the lead in a short film and playing small roles in indie feature films.

I still have a big list of goals left. I have the dream that so many of us have of a "proper part on the telly" so that all my school friends and relatives can be impressed and tell their friends that they know me. The industry works in such a vague way that I don't know which of my many endeavours will lead to this, or whether it will even happen. I have other goals though, and I know that as long as I can keep acting and making things, getting a sub-five-liner on The Bill won't make or break me.

Sometimes it's useful to have a big goal to aim for and mine is to have a good part in a great film. (I will also accept a great part in a good film.) I've set a rough timeline of five years for this, but who knows? It might take ten, or twenty. Over the last two years I've discovered lots of different strategies for getting there so as long as I keep working and learning, it doesn't really matter how long it takes.

In many ways the future is entirely impossible to predict. There are so many great opportunities, new ideas and fabulous people to collaborate with that what most amazes me about the last two years are all the things that I had no idea would happen. By doing them once I know I can do them again, and I also know that I'll be able to do more new things that I can't even imagine yet.

In the grand scheme of your life, two years is not a long time. Acting is one of the most rewarding activities that you can undertake and if you long to do it then that's a clue that you should give it a try. With so many evening classes, fringe productions and people to collaborate with, it's never been easier to get started and have fun. Online casting sites have opened up the industry, so you don't need to be with an exclusive agent to get a big break and if you are persistent you can build a career on your own, while still having time to earn a living from something else.

The more that you try things the more ideas will come to you. Do a class and you might meet a potential collaborator. See a show and you might get an idea for a webseries that you can self-shoot on a mobile. The possibilities are endless and everything is cumulative – the more you do, the more you learn and the more opportunities open up for you.

Taking up acting has completely transformed my life. I am more fulfilled, I have better relationships with people, I am able to do my day job better and I am heading closer towards the goal of self-actualisation. And it all started with an entry level class at City Lit. Maybe you should give it a go too.

APPENDIX:
BOOKS AND ONLINE RESOURCES

There are a fantastic number of books and resources able to help you on your journey. Here I've listed all the ones that have helped me but this list is not exhaustive (and is London-centric). Look for more resources with a Google search, or by joining online groups and asking people you meet at events.

Books

You can read books about all aspects of acting. There are enough books written that I'm sure you could start reading them all now and keep going until you die without ever stopping to actually do any acting. Don't do that!

I find books useful as a way to get new ideas or to gee myself up to get on with doing something more productive. Here is a selection of those I have found most useful.

The Artists Way by Julia Cameron
The Artists Way is the book that started me on the journey to become an actor. Simple, quiet, kind and deeply penetrating this

book will work for you if you have time to engage with the exercises and are willing to open your heart and do things differently.

Big Magic by Elizabeth Gilbert

I think of Big Magic as a more accessible version of The Artists Way. Another full-time artist, Elizabeth Gilbert understands the same deep truths as Julia Cameron but puts them in a more light-hearted (and less religious!) way.

Impro by Keith Johnston

Keith Johnston did a lot of amazing work around improvisation and acting with the subconscious mind. This book opened my eyes to the idea that my best acting might come from a place that I can't logically control or train. It's a fascinating read.

Different every night by Mike Alfreds

Different every night is a great take on what makes a good actor, written by director Mike Alfreds. I read this book very early on and I found it useful for guiding what I was aiming for in learning to become an actor.

An Actor Prepares by Constantin Stanislavsky

Stanislavsky needs no introduction. This is one of the most widely read books in the world of acting. It's fun to read nowadays, particularly to get the nice warm glow of realisation that few modern directors will treat you quite as badly as the fictional director in Stanislavsky's book. This is not a set of instructions to be followed slavishly but it is definitely useful as a source of ideas about acting.

The Sedona Method by Hale Dwoskin

The Sedona Method is a self-help tool for releasing unhelpful emotions. This is great for calming pre-audition or performance nerves. Further I think the usefulness of this book for the actor actually extends beyond this – as an actor your job is to channel emotions and making your peace with feeling angry, desolate and despairing is a necessary step towards that.

Lo-to-no Budget Film-making by Elliot Grove

If you are interested in taking up acting more seriously, I strongly recommend making your own work. Putting on a play can be done for minimal cost, but shooting a film often feels more unapproachable. This is a great book to learn about all aspects of film-making and how to achieve a big budget look for low budget investment.

I, An Actor by Nicholas Craig

If all of this serious acting reading has got too much for you, take a break by reading "I, An Actor". Written by Nigel Planer (of The Young Ones) and Christopher Douglas, this spoof of an actor's biography will help you to laugh at how much of the industry remains silly and self-regarding.

Inspiration

Wendy Braun – Actor Inspiration

When I was starting out as an actor, I was feeling low and searching for inspiration on the internet. Typing in "Actor inspiration" I found Wendy Braun's site for actors - **http://actorinspiration.com/**.

There are many lovely messages on Wendy's site and in her weekly email. She reminds her subscribers time and time again that the important thing is to become happy first, and then professional success will follow. Whether you believe this or not, it's great advice to follow since even if it doesn't work you do as a minimum end up happy!

My first reaction, which I suspect is not uncommon, is "yes, well it's alright for you to say that Wendy Braun – you've already got a Hollywood career!". You'll get the most out of this site when you realise that the "happy first" approach applies to everyone, not just people who have more experience than you. In the world of acting, whatever credits you get are never enough and you are always chasing more. I find this site a great way to remember that if you're not happy while you're doing it – what's the point?

Anthony Meindl

Anthony Meindl was recommended to me by a fellow actor on the London Actors Workshop course. He's a terribly inspiring chap who writes books and articles to help you to get along in the world of acting. He runs classes in LA and all around the world.

He's published three books:

- **AT LEFT BRAIN TURN RIGHT**
- **Alphabet Soup for Grown-Ups**
- **BOOK THE F#©KING JOB!**

Find out about all of these at **http://www.anthonymeindl.com/**.

Casting Websites

The great innovation of modern times is peer to peer interactions on the internet. If you were trying to audition fifty years ago, you wouldn't be able to get an audition unless you had an agent or you managed to doorstep the casting director. Similarly, if you'd been trying to cast for a short film, you could only have found actors through agents and would have been charged a hefty premium.

Nowadays the system has been enhanced by the creation of many, many online casting sites. Downsides are that the same jobs will be posted on multiple sites and there is still a layer of "top jobs" that aren't posted on these sites at all. The number of actors on these site compared to the number of roles is very high. So you will get invited to audition for only a fraction of the roles that you apply for, and they may be auditioning a large number of people meaning that you are then unlikely to get the role.

There are a large number of sites out there, and I recommend having a look to find which ones work for you. Extras agencies can also be great to get experience on large film sets. These are the sites that I use.

Casting Call Pro
Casting Call Pro is the second most used and respected site after Spotlight. Unlike Spotlight, there are no criteria in order for you to be able to join, you simply hand over your money and get started.

Most of the work on CCP is unpaid, which is great if you are starting out. Beware of the difference between a student film and an unpaid professional short. You are likely to get much better showreel material and experience on the latter (although having said that I've had some great experiences on student films).

http://castingcallpro.com/uk/

Shooting People

Shooting People is my absolute favourite website. It is a community resource for all people interested in starting out in film production: directors, editors, camera people etc. This means that it is a site where actors are in the minority (although more actors are now realising that and joining up!).

On SP you can get advice on making your own short film or web series, as well as casting notices for other people's film projects. SP is also much more affordable than a lot of the websites that are targeted at actors.

http://shootingpeople.org

Spotlight

Spotlight is the big daddy of all casting websites. In order to maintain its position as an elite resource, you must meet eligibility criteria before you can join as an actor. For many actors who are starting out, collecting credits so that you can register with Spotlight is the first game you play.

Spotlight doesn't post unpaid jobs, and most of the casting calls you'll receive are for commercials, corporate work or musical theatre. I have never had an audition via Spotlight, but I belong because it shows that I am a professional. I have heard that top level jobs are posted via Spotlight but only to (specific) agencies.

http://spotlight.com

Courses

City Lit

City Lit run a vast selection of courses for adults. Their drama department is well established and offers courses ranging from weekend and evening introductory classes, to specialist improvers classes to 1,2 and 3 year accredited drama courses.

I did my first ever adult acting class at City Lit and it gave me the confidence to continue on my journey. You can see a list of what they offer at **http://www.citylit.ac.uk/courses/performing-arts/acting-and-theatre.**

London Actors Workshop

I was recommended the London Actors Workshop by a friend who had completed it a few years before. Since then I've been amazing how many other actors I meet have also done the 12-week introductory course.

The London Actors Workshop combines a whistlestop tour of acting (Improvisation, Method Acting, TV & Film Acting, Sight Reading, Audition technique, Screen Combat and Text Analysis) with three casting director meetings and an industry showcase. It's a great combination of skills training plus an opportunity to learn about the industry and how to get ahead.

Off the back of the industry showcase, I was invited to audition with an agency (which I blew, but that wasn't LAW's fault!) and I met loads of great friends on the course.

The course runs every three months. You can see details at **http://londonactorsworkshop.co.uk/**. It's very popular so the next course is often fully booked, but you can usually sign up for the one in three months' time.

RADA over 24s

Did you know that RADA offers evening classes for over 24s? I couldn't believe it when I found out and yes, I am now a RADA-trained actor. The classes are hotter than tickets to see Madonna and you need to be signed up to their mailing list in order to be notified about when tickets go on sale. If you want to sign up to the most popular class "Introduction to Acting", you'll need to be waiting by your browser when the tickets go on-sale in order to snap up a place.

They offer classes on a variety of topics. I have studied Shakespeare and text analysis in their "Masterclass" sessions. Something else that can be fun to do is their Shakespeare Awards – you are assessed on two pieces of pre-prepared Shakespeare. I did the Bronze level last year and plan to have a stab at Silver when I get a lull in my other work.

Take a look at **https://www.rada.ac.uk/education-and-outreach/adult-evening-acting-classes-over-24s/introduction** to see what is available and to sign up to the mailing list.

Actors Centre

The Actors Centre is an organisation in central London that supports actors throughout their careers. They run short courses on any topic you can imagine – several each day. They also have a café and a theatre in their Covent Garden home, and the theatre has slots specially put aside for members to mount their shows.

I did the best course I have ever taken at the Actors Centre – Script to Screen, a five day film acting course that culminated in our shooting a complete short film – and I have put on two productions at The Tristan Bates Theatre (part of the Actors Centre). Every year they run a Festival of Solo Performance, which is a great place to try out your first solo show. (I did!)

Because the Actors Centre is for professional actors only, they do have criteria that you need to meet in order to become a member. Another hurdle to jump when you are starting out! I only realised after I had joined that in fact they offer several classes to non-members and while they do not guarantee that you can join if you complete one of these classes, I understand that they will assess your suitability and may let you join.

Check out the options at **https://www.actorscentre.co.uk/non-members**.

the salon:collective

the salon:collective is a fantastic organisation that specialises in training in the Meisner technique. I am currently doing their level 2 Meisner training, having come across the organisation by acting in a play with one of their alumni.

They currently offer Meisner, Shakespeare, Voice and Physical Theatre training. Details at **http://thesaloncollective.org/**.

People

I've been helped on my journey by individuals who have a special talent for nurturing new actors and I list a few of them here. It's important when you are starting out to think carefully about who you choose to work with. Look hard for authenticity, positivity and people who are giving rather than taking. If someone makes you feel bad for being inexperienced, move on and work with someone else. Life is too short.

Peta Lily

Peta Lily is a performer, director and teacher. She has created a new, deep body of acting work called Dark Clown and she teaches this, along with theatre workshops and masterclasses.

I worked with Peta on my one-woman show "Dark Dates: An Audience with Cassandra Bick" and it was a fabulous experience. Peta has an incomparable ability to inspire you to work your hardest through an understanding and gentle approach, which is especially useful if you are an inexperienced actor.

Sign up to her mailing list and find out about her classes at **http://www.petalily.com/**.

Jeremy Stockwell

Jeremy Stockwell is a unique performer, director and coach. Often described as a philosopher, Jeremy has a fantastic perspective on life and acting that helps you move from simply acting to living truthfully in the moment.

Jeremy is a senior tutor at RADA and also gives short courses and private coaching. He has been my coach for eighteen months and I couldn't recommend him more highly. Get in touch with him via his website **http://www.jeremystockwell.co.uk/**.

Amelie Mettenheimer

Amelie Mettenheimer is an acting coach who specialises in helping European actors who are looking to move to LA. I very much hope to need this service one day.

Amelie gave me some amazing advice early on in my career. When I said that I hadn't yet been on stage because I hadn't been accepted from an audition, she said "Don't give me that nonsense! Go and put on a one-woman show."

She gives classes in the UK and US, does one to one coaching and has other resources on her website: **http://www.ameliemettenheimer.com/**.

Zoe Cunningham has trained as an actor at RADA, The Actors Centre and City Lit. She acted in her first one woman show at the Tristan Bates Theatre in February 2015 to critical acclaim and subsequently toured the show to Brighton Fringe. Other theatre credits include Mrs Arbuthnot in Oscar Wilde's a Woman of No Importance and social worker Moira in Chris Lee's modern work Shallow Slumber. On film she has appeared opposite Steve Coogan and Anna Friel in Michael Winterbottom's The Look of Love, and has played Clara, a confidence trickster, in indie Brit-flick Carbon Foxes.